Distilling Creativity

or

How to live your Highly Creative life and not die trying.

Dr P.H. Court

DISTILLING CREATIVITY

Cataloguing-in-Publication entry is available from the National Library of Australia http:/catalogue.nla.gov.au/.

This edition first published in Hackham, South Australia by Immortalise via Ingram Spark in August 2024.
www.immortalise.com.au

ISBN 978-0-6459991-7-4

Typesetting and cover by Ben Morton

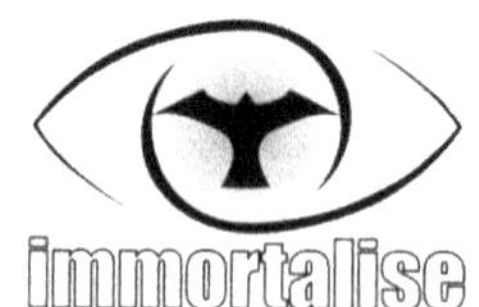

Acknowledgements

This book is the result of years developing, teaching, learning and sharing the creative journey at Tabor College Adelaide. Many brilliant students have shaped my thinking, added new wrinkles and opened my eyes. Turning all that wonder into a book has been the work of many years and many mothers. My Dad, Dr John Court first pushed me in and then helped me stay afloat. Justine, who has provided more than just wisdom and unconditional support. Dr James Cooper who lets me run rampant in his Creative Writing program. Ben Morton, publisher and guiding light and Esther Cremona who was a student, is now a teacher, and a fine professional proofreader. Any errors are mine because I probably ignored her. Beyond these people is a sea of brilliant humans who have ridden this rollercoaster with me in radio, television, writing and just living this creative life. I thank you all.

Also by PH Court through Stone Table Books

Sub Urban Tales

The Used Men's Bicycle Club (and other stories from the end of the world.)

'Funny, deftly strange, PH Court's stories slide from chaotic and overwhelming to satirical. When he nails it, it's hard to stop reading.'

The Advertiser

Contact:

phcourt.author@gmail.com

phcourt.com

Stone Table Books

editor@stonetablebooks.com

www.stonetablebooks.com

What the hell do YOU know?

You've picked up a book about being highly creative so presumably it's something you care about. Personally. Otherwise you'd be flicking through Insta or TikTok or whatever the webternet is this week. You care about your creativity and you're willing to put some effort into understanding it.

You and me both.

But why listen to me? I mean, there are dozens and dozens of blogs and books about being creative, by really well known, well respected, highly creative people. Many of those books and those people will get a mention in here but there's a problem with most of those books.

The highly creative person writes a book about what *they* do, what makes *them* create and how *they* have lived their best and worst creative life. But they are not me. They are not you. We are all different and maybe some of us are more different than others.

If I want a book that helps *me*, the best thing to do is write my own book. The best thing for *you,* however, is if someone digs through all those other books, all the research, the reams, and years of knowledge, and then distils it all down into a set of simple understandings that relate to us all. In other words, a book that looks not at the unique individual, but at the common, the uniform, the things that matter to *all* of us. And that's what I have done. Distilled creativity.

Which leads to two very important questions. What the hell do I know? And why did I do this book this way?

Let's start with the hard truths. I failed at school. I was terrible. I didn't flunk my last year; I completely missed it. I didn't even get to sit exams or hand up final work. I just disappeared. School and I agreed to go our separate ways and never speak to each other again. When I should have been knuckling down to study and doing assignments, I was busy. I had a 'job'. Unlike most school kids in Australia, I was working on TV. I was selected, in my final year, to be part of a national TV show called *Kids Only*, and then *Klips*, which screened across the nation to weary school kids arriving home to cold lime cordial and peanut butter toast. I was selected from a national search of schools and was found to be "Bright and Breezy," according to the local paper. I was just a kid, chucked into this massive media machine and convinced I was there because I deserved it. And then it ended. I was a failed, unemployed child star. I put that on my resumé and ended up being a waiter for a few years. Not a good waiter, but I got paid.

Anyway, this isn't a memoir, so let me hit the salient points. I eventually found my way into community radio. Then commercial radio. My first commercial radio gig was as production manager at a talk station. Yes, straight in at manager! I was making adverts in a multitrack production studio. I had never even *seen* a multitrack production studio before I walked in for my first day. It was make or break time so, day one, I took out all the manuals for all the gear and read like a mad man. It still took me many months to master this new world, but I did. Most of the folk at radio *5AA* have no idea that I had no idea what I was doing. It was there I learned my first lesson. Always learn everything you can and make sure you know what to do when things don't work.

Later I began writing radio comedy pieces for that station which got me into the behemoth *Austereo* network where I would write, direct and produce comedy content for their entire FM network. I managed a team of half a dozen creative folk and we churned out mountains of excellent radio comedy. And some crap. I worked with some of the highest rated radio shows in Australian media history and had more than my fair share of impact. From there I went into advertising for a while as a creative director, copy writer and running my own creative consultancy. The problem with advertising is, there's a burst of creativity followed by mind numbing mounds of mundane waiting about for others to make up their minds. So I got back into radio. This time as breakfast host. I was blessed to work with really talented and totally humble folk who, like me, loved pumping out tons of great fun. In the advertising agency I might have a week to come up with a killer concept. On live radio, that song ends in two minutes and fifteen seconds, and you better have something stunning to say and do. *That's* living. A breakfast radio show is three hours of blasting along at reckless speed with your pants on fire, whilst sounding and being calm, relaxed, and friendly. I loved it. And I thrived at it. I mentored others and shared what I had learned. And then I went to university.

At the age of 35 I decided to do a Bachelor of Media degree. I figured I could learn what I didn't know. Long story short, I convinced the world I could study now, despite failing miserably at school, and I started a run of degrees that included media, psychology and creative writing. All whilst creating a pile of award-winning short stories, magazine publications and novels. ABC TV unknowingly paid for a lot of my undergrad years because I was writing freelance for their *Backberner* satirical TV show. I also continued to work in radio and advertising whilst proving that I really could be a good student.

When I ended my university career, naturally, I went back to university. I was writing a novel, so I decided to turn it into a PhD in creative writing. Then I was invited to help rebuild a master's program in creative writing. The first thing we did was fix the huge hole in academic creative writing study. That is; nowhere, in all my decades of study in creative writing, had anyone bothered to explain what 'Creative' actually is and how to do it.

I spent five years building a subject that is now core to a *Masters of Creative Writing and Communication.* That subject is called *Thriving Creativity.* Originally it was called *Surviving Creativity* but, as students noted, this tended to focus on the negative. The course, and this book, are designed to positively help *you* find *your* creative life. Not mine, not anyone else's, just you.

So what the hell do I know? Only what I know. When I started studying media, after twenty years running media at the highest commercial levels, I was constantly saying 'Ooooh, so *that's* why I do that.' I knew stuff. I just didn't know what it was and why. When it comes to your creative life, you will know stuff too. Maybe it will be different stuff. That's why I love teaching this. I learn something every day. And that's why I am happy to invite you to join me as we walk through this thing. Because there's nothing better than learning by doing. And that's what makes it worthwhile for both of us.

So what are we doing here?

To hear some people talk, you'd think being consistently creative is either weird, lethal, or impossible. And yet, every human being is, as we'll see, creative. Where do we get these negative ideas from and why? Why would Professor Kay Redfield Jamison say that 'A common assumption... is that within artistic circles madness is somehow normal.' (4) What makes Margaret Boden, in her book *The Creative Mind,* suggest that 'In the abstract however, creativity can seem utterly impossible, even less to be expected than unicorns.' (29) Why is creativity so massively misunderstood? How can there be so much research into it, and yet so many of us still find it so baffling?

The answer is actually pretty simple. And logical.

Creativity and its results are incredibly diverse. Because it comes from humans, and humans are incredibly diverse. So we all have a unique way of doing it. Creativity becomes a problem when I do the equivalent of putting high octane rocket fuel in my cheerful little Toyota. It won't turn my average street car into a roaring racing machine. It will likely turn it into a news story involving the fire service and neighbours saying, 'he seemed like such a quiet boy and then BOOM'. By the same token if I tried to perform like, for example, the late Robin Williams, I would fail miserably. Why? Because I'm less creative than he was? Because he was riding some miraculous fireball? No.

Simply because I'm *not* Robin Williams. And he was never me. Watching Robin Williams at work, it is clear that he is using the same skills, the same creative resources I use. The same creative elements that we all use. But he is using them differently, uniquely. He is doing it his way. And so are you. So am I. If I try to fuel my creativity with someone else's fuel, I'm going to explode. Or burn out. Or just... fail.

If you have ever wanted to expand your creative talents, to explore the natural ups and downs, and explain to yourself what is actually happening when you create, then we are going to get along just fine, because that is exactly what I want for you too. This is a book that wants you to burn, not burn out. To create with explosive joy and passion, rather than just blowing up.

The book is a distilled collection of really interesting, often weird but always powerful observations about the life and work of highly creative people. But it is also leaning on the reasoned and researched delving of some very wise academic and scientific thinkers. There are quotes and viewpoints from creative people you'll know and maybe some you won't. You will find inspiration and suggestions for you to apply to your own life. But they won't all fit. There will be many things that you will find here that will make you roll your eyes and say things like 'you have no idea how my life works!' And that's true. Which is why you can feel free to pick and choose. Try some things out and if they don't work for you, that's not bad. That's reality. But keep going, find the things that will help you bring your creativity to life.

All the work has been condensed down and distilled down to help you, personally, individually, to unravel the myth and mystery of your own creative life and help you find your way to thrive. It won't tell you what to think but it might well help you work out what to think about.

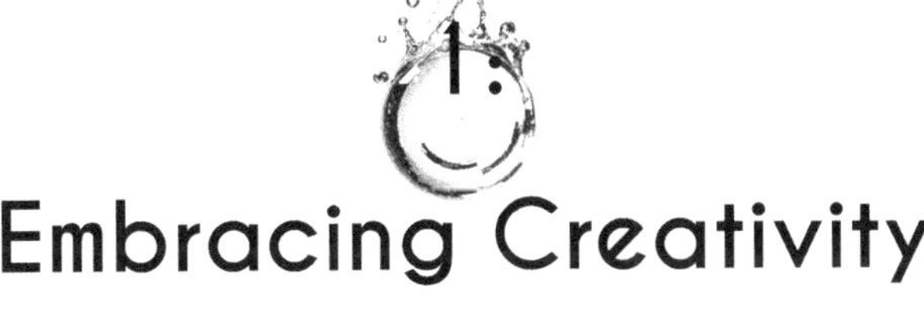

1: Embracing Creativity

What it is... or is it?

> Everyone thinks writers must know more about the inside of the human head, but that is wrong. They know less, that's why they write. Trying to find out what everyone else takes for granted. (37)
>
> MARGARET ATWOOD

When I started thinking about creativity, my dad threw me a curveball. This is a problem since he is an Englishman and therefore useless at baseball. He was a fine cricketer in his time so perhaps "My dad threw me a wrong 'un". But Englishmen don't 'throw' wrong 'uns. That's frowned upon in cricket. See how difficult a simple thing like a creative metaphor can become? Anyway, I was chatting with my dad about this creativity lark. I'm blessed to be surrounded by highly regarded psychological thinkers. (More on how he changed my creative thinking later.) He pointed out that everything seems to have an antonym. In order to exist, things tend to have an opposite. Dark and light, happiness and grief, up and down, creativity and... um...

So what *is* the opposite of creativity? Plagiarism? Not really because all creation comes from somewhere, drawing on past experience. Like Thomas Newcomen, who invented the atmospheric engine when 'he took a whole lot of other people's ideas and built them into a single engine.' (Bell, 82) His creative collation would lead to the steam engine and the first industrial revolution. It's the same with any creative product. It's frequently made up of things and ideas that already exist. Therefore, the line between stealing someone else's work or creatively reframing it in a unique way can be a question that keeps lawyers in expensive suits.

Perhaps the opposite of creativity is predictability? Except another of the defining factors of effective creativity is that, once created, the creation can often seem to have been so obvious it's a wonder no one thought of it before. 'OMG, it's so obvious, now that we see it.' Japanese author Hyuki Murakami thrives in the understanding that there's nothing really unique about himself. He notes 'I'm not intelligent. I'm not arrogant. I'm just like the people who read my books.' (354) Maya Angelou also highlights how the very pinnacle of creative output for her is to seem as if it is nothing at all.

> I have to have my writing so polished that it doesn't look polished at all. I want a reader, especially an editor, to be a half-hour into my book before he realizes it's reading he's doing. (263)

So, is blandness the opposite of creativity? Possibly. But Joan London leans heavily on the life ordinary for her creative time, saying 'I do distrust being too excited about my work. I prefer a medium, sort of just-keep-going, don't-go-up-and-don't-go-down state.' (251) Her work is far from bland. Besides, surely blandness is a matter of taste? Creativity is a matter of... um... what *is* creativity a matter of?

It seems fascinating, at such an early stage of this book, to run aground on so many contradictory questions of definition. And this, my fellow travellers, is one of the reasons why creativity is seen as such a mysterious, fraught, tumultuous thing. Derick Pao puts it like this:

> Therein lies the beauty and secret of creativity that perhaps can never be fully explained or analyzed. "The moment of Aha!" is not only elusive, but one can never be sure of when, or how, or exactly where it really comes from. (vii)

But creativity is a thing, right? Surely it can be defined? And yet, when she was writing her book *The Creative Mind*, Margaret Boden realised that:

> A psychological explanation of creativity, it seems, is in principle unachievable. It is not even clear that there can possibly be anything for it to explain. – And yet, undeniably, there is. (2)

Or, as John Hoorn points out, 'There is no standard to decide what is creative.' (237) It seems the problem is this. Yes, creativity exists. But it's hard to put it in a nice measurable, replicable, scientifically robust box. This makes it really hard for researchers to deal with because 'It just is' doesn't look good on a data set. However, since this is not a scientific manual and since we don't want to plough through reams of statistical data, the definition we need for creativity is a practical one, not a technical one. If this book was about gravity, it would not bother with the theorems of force and mass and the endless explanatory algorithms. It would simply say 'gravity is what makes things fall if you drop them.' It's a working definition. This definition may be a bit simplistic if you work in a science lab, but if you are a creative person seeking to understand what it means to create, you just need a solid, logical definition of what it is we are actually discussing, right? So, here we go.

A working definition of human creativity:

Some very famous people have bent their creative brains to this and come up with things like this, from the legendary comic genius John Cleese, who states in his book, cunningly titled, *Creativity:* 'By creativity, I simply mean new ways of thinking about things.' (3)

Well, that's a start. But there are people medicated in quiet rooms who try to drill holes in their own heads because they have 'new ways of thinking about things.' We don't call this creativity. We call this psychosis. When the 'new ways of thinking about things' are troubling and ruin your life, that is a condition that needs professional help. Is it 'creativity'? Well, I'm going to say yes. But. And it's a big but. But; in order for creativity to be a useful thing, to have some value in the world, it needs an extra little something. In 1986, Joseph Renzulli tried to explain what creativity meant when he was talking about gifted kids. He came up with:

> Creative– productive giftedness… describes those aspects of human activity [which involve] original thought, solutions, material, and products that are purposefully designed to have an impact on one or more target audiences…[and] emphasise the use and application of information (content) and thinking

> processes in an integrated, inductive, and real-problem-oriented manner… (255)

Sorry if you had to read that twice. It's not as simple as John Cleese, but it does point to 'solutions' and being 'purposefully designed'. It also highlights that creativity is original thought, based on learning and applied in a real, problem solving manner. Nice. While I'm not sure making up a knock-knock joke is 'real-problem-solving' oriented, I would consider it to be creative. Can't creativity occur without a 'need' for it? Chetan Walia is an academic too, but his definition of creativity looks less like legal jargon. He says that:

> …the creative process is not directly observable and this makes it a difficult subject to study… Herein lies the problem in studying creativity as synonymous with creation, because creation can be judged only when it has concluded, whereas creativity is active throughout the process and may not even end after having led to creation. (238-239)

So, creativity is hard to see until there is a creation that has emerged from this creativity. But is that putting the cart before the invention of the horse? Before we can understand our creative output, don't we want to know what creativity actually is? Let's turn away from the scientists and hear from Rich Gold who was a philosophical chap. His book *The Plenitude* looked at the place of things and stuff in the modern world. This is what he thinks creativity is:

> At its core, I maintain, it simply means making stuff that has never been made before, that nobody has even thought of before and is not a warmed over replica of something already made. It could be an idea, or a concept, or a string of words. (53-54)

What is interesting here is that all those scientists are looking at creativity scientifically. Rich Gold is looking at it commercially. They are considering how it can be measured, he is looking at the saleable product created. But what of those who consider creativity as an artistic thing, not a solely commercial output? Tom McLeish compared creativity in poets, and creativity as expressed by scientists, and threw in the consideration that creativity is;

> … the outward and explosive force of the imagination being met and formed into something true and beautiful by the world's constraints. (2)

The idea of an 'Outward explosive force of the imagination' that then gets worked on and shaped, feels like a powerful explanation of creativity. But such neatness and clarity is thrown under a bus by people like Sakavat Mammadov, suggesting that:

> Creativity is a multifaceted and complex construct over which there has been a long history of disagreement among creativity psychologists. Although there is not a standard definition of creativity, most of the definitions converge in their agreement that creativity is the process of producing something both original and valuable. (174)

So, kind of a 'We don't really know but there's probably something about originality and being valuable.' By now we're all pretty much over all these quotes and incomplete considerations so let me try and land this plane in a way that will give us a useful definition of what our creativity actually is. Ernest Hemingway, who could write a bit, speaks of his creativity being like a well. 'Trying to write something of permanent value is a full time job,' (13) he says, and then nails down exactly how he did that:

> The well is where your "juice" is. Nobody knows what it is made of, least of all yourself. What you know is if you have it, or you have to wait for it to come back. (19)

Sorry, that's not very helpful. Yet. Hemingway knows what it is, but he doesn't know what it is. Spoken like a true writer. But believe it or not, we're actually getting somewhere here. This 'well' that Hemingway was drawing from will come up later as we look at how to thrive creatively, because it is a nice metaphor for the beginning of your creativity. Which leads to the obvious conclusion. Creativity *comes* from somewhere. This is a very important point. As Jonathon Kladder notes:

> Across the literature, a clear theme exists: creativity is more about slow, tedious, and hard work than a single moment of insight. (403)

Ah, so perhaps it's not all about the flash and craziness. It's about something that comes from somewhere and goes somewhere. Even more, Kladder describes creativity as 'tedious'. This is not a common impression of the creative life. "So Mr Spielberg, how would you describe your process? Oh, it's tedious really." But hold on to the 'tedious' idea, it may prove helpful later. And it moves us closer to a useful definition of what we do. If you want a really deeply researched dive into the whole subject, find six months to read Jeff and Julia Crabtree's Book *Living with a Creative Mind.* In it you'll find this nugget:

> Creativity is a process. It is not a thing; nor is it magic or mystery. It is a process that is dynamic and fluid and never occurs in isolation. Because it is a process, we can work out what parts there are to it- and we can work out what things either fuel or frustrate it. (18)

Now it starts to make more sense. One big reason psychology, research, culture and history have had trouble defining creativity is because it's an ongoing thing. It's not even a single thing. It is a process. The very English writer William Somerset Maugham explains his process like this. 'I have always liked to let things simmer in my mind for a long time before setting them down on paper.' (31)

Let's add another thought. For clarity and simplicity, I want to head to the digital realm and find British educator and philosopher, the late Sir Ken Robinson presenting one of the most viewed TED talks ever. He defines creativity for his enraptured audience like this.

Creativity is having original ideas that have value.

Isn't that nice? So simple and concise. I can understand creativity like that. But, let me just tweak it a little. For the sake of this book and with the aim of helping creative people become better and more effective at being creative, I'll throw all these things into a blender, the complex and the simple, and produce this single, concise definition of creativity.

Creativity comes from within and is a process from which original ideas develop a product that has value.

Well, that seems to sum up creativity nicely. It is thought, so it comes from the human mind. It is original, so it's something that has not necessarily been conceptually available before in this form. It is a process, so it takes place over time and trials. And it leads to something being produced and, finally, that product has value.

Notice I removed Joseph Kladder's 'Tedious'. That's because I have actually learned to love the process, the work, the ongoing labour that is creativity. Personally, I don't find it tedious anymore. Quite the opposite. As we shall see later, the compulsion to create and be creative means that pursuing it can become central to who I am. And I like to think I'm not too tedious.

So, this is a definition that works *for me.* For you, this may have holes. Maybe, like Joseph Kladder, you want to include 'tedious' in your definition. Maybe your passion leads you to focus on some different aspect. That's okay. This is just the basis *for me*, and an encouragement for you to develop you own functional definition of what *your* creativity is. For example, perhaps you find this definition runs aground on the word 'value'. For the psychotic patient in the hospital trying to get the aliens out of his head with a drill, the value is clear. To him. The value is to get peace from the terrible things in his own head. To sit in a meadow and ponder the unravelling nature of clouds has enormous value. To the individual. Staring down a microscope in search of 'what the heck is happening here' is of value, perhaps to all mankind. Sitting in a glass and chrome office with people called Tarquin, throwing around concepts for an advertising campaign has value. Dollar value. And maybe little else. And on and on it goes. The value of a creative thought or even a creative action may be intrinsic to itself, that is, it's a 'good idea', or brings a personal value. Or its value can be extrinsic. The creation of a song, a story, a scientific equation or an advertising jingle that reaches into the world.

Does it matter WHAT the value is?

No, not really. And yes, yes it does, because the value we place on our creative output will determine how much we invest in it and how much we seek it and expand it. What happens to our creativity will deeply inform who we think we are and what is the value of our ideas. That will have a huge impact on you, the creator. Finding out what creativity means *to you* will become very important. In the following chapters we'll have a look at some of the correlations between being creative and being mentally broken. We'll break down some of the stereotypes and reframe how to think about creativity so you can use it wisely. Because it is possible that living a highly creative life, whilst setting many of us free, can actually drive some off the deep end. When looking at the mental health of highly creative folk, for example, Janelle Hallaert and her team found that;

> ...professional artists (defined using standard federal occupational codes which included visual, performance, music, and literary careers) had a 125% higher risk for suicide than non-artists when gender and sociodemographic variables were controlled. The

> percentage increased to 270% when those variables were included. (335)

Clearly, something is going on here. These are really substantial findings and so, if you want to live and thrive in your creative life, you need to be aware of what's at stake. Or, as another couple of researchers put it:

> What most studies have shown, therefore, is that those in arts are more likely to be mentally ill than those in other professions. Writers are, generally, more likely to be mentally ill and die young than others in the arts. Poets are the most at risk of them all, with higher rates of mental illness, suicide, and mortality than other writers, other artists, and the general population. (Kaufman and Sexton, 270)

The simple fact is this. Creativity is a vital part of being human, and it is something we need to get a handle on if we want to tame the fire and burn bright without burning up. It's like love. As the cynical folk say 'You can't live with it and you can't live without it.' Mihaly Csikszentmihalyi who, as well as having a killer surname, crystalised the concept of creative 'flow', notes that highly functioning creativity emerges from an autotelic function. Autotelic creativity, in this sense is,

> ...a self-contained activity, one that is done not with the expectation of some future benefit, but simply because the doing itself is the reward. (67)

We create because we love to create. Because it is who we are. If we are created to be creators then it is vital that we understand the inner workings of this creative drive, how we use it, and how it can use us.

A word about...
This thing as a 'Cult?'

Samuel Franklin's much lauded 2023 book *The Cult of Creativity* makes some very interesting observations about the appropriation, monetisation and social constructionism applied to 'Creative' work and creativity as a concept. In short, his thesis is that from the 1950's psychology, science, business and government decided that creativity would be the way forward for the development of the democratic western world. 50 years prior, in a 1970 article entitled *Creativity: Cult: Myth,* Professor George K Stark was saying the same thing, explaining how the great 'Holy Creativity', as he calls it, came about;

> We know that the crusading medicine show [of creativity] brilliantly incorporated psychologists, scientists, mathematicians, financiers, clerics, sociologists, anthropologists, civil servants, philosophers, historians, et. El, hypnotized with "The Great Potential." (219)

Samuel Franklin goes a little deeper and is a little more involved than that, and worth a read if you're interested. But the idea suggested by both works, is that creativity became a thing in post war western society. Of course, that's not true. There has always been a wealth of creativity and creation happening. In fact, it could be suggested that the first thing that ever happened was Creation. Since then, there has been a wealth of it occurring. Sometimes it was called invention, ideas, inspirations, imagination, fluffy thinking, or any number of other terms used before the worlds of academia and publishing began to tame the concept by putting a shirt named 'creativity' on it. Like I say, it's an interesting book, but even if the term 'creativity' wasn't a big thing until the 50's, the fact of it, and what being that inventive, imaginative force means to you and me as individuals, that hasn't changed at all. You'll notice that this book in your hands right now has spent a lot of time exploring what the term 'Creativity' means and how difficult it is to nail down. In the light of Mr Franklin's hand wringing anxiety that creativity may have become ensnared in the military industrial complex, or whatever is the concern of the day, I stand by my claim; that as an individual who has a heart and mind created by a creator God, it's really important that you work out for yourself what 'creativity' means to you, personally, in your life and in your time.

Stark, George. Creativity: Cult: Myth. *Improving College and University Teaching,* Vol 18. No. 3. (Summer). Pp. 219-221. 1970

Franklin, Samuel. *Cult of Creativity. A Surprisingly Recent History.* University of Chicago Press. 2023

Who is creative?

And how?

People have said to me 'Oh, I'm not creative' or 'I'm not really *that* creative.' Can you hear yourself saying that? Well, stop it. It's like saying 'Oh, I'm no good at cooking.' Maybe you're not skilled at a particular cuisine or you may burn toast whilst it's still in the bag. But you eat, you prepare food, somehow, somewhere. So you *can* cook. Anyone *can* cook if we learn, practice and enjoy it. You might only be able to put milk on the cereal. Claim that! It won't get you your own TV show but at least you won't starve to death. By the same token, *anyone* can be, and is, creative. 'I'm not creative' is one of the biggest lies we tell ourselves. Why this lie is so common, we'll look at later, but for now let me explain how you can know that you *are* creative.

A lot of researchers have spent decades running this little puppy we call creativity through its paces and have come up with some very robust results. Let me just stop there and point out that, in the world of psychological research 'robust results' are as rare as a rock-solid metaphor for something really rare. The nature of variance and difference in human individuals, across cultures, language groups, ages, and eras, makes a 'robust finding' nearly impossible. So much is variable in human existence that to find something that looks like a universal truth is mind blowing. But here it is. Using its super high tech mega academic name, the amazing thing is:

The Be Creative Effect.

The research and re-research on this have been going on in papers and journals since the late 50's at least. (Christensen, et al) but let me just give you the cut down layman's version:

The most common version of the experiment that explores The Be Creative Effect is the Alternative Uses Task, develop by Liam Hudson and others in the late 60's. Being science we give it a TLA (Three Letter Acronym) and call it the AUT. The AUT is simple. A group of people (usually a classroom of bored university undergrads) get split into two groups and then shown a common, boring object. Let's say it's a brick. (Sorry if you find bricks fascinating, just stay focused here.)

Half the class is told to come up with as many *Different* uses for a brick as they can. The second group is told to *Be Creative* and come up with as many *Unique* uses for a brick as they can. Given some time, the individuals, or sometimes in groups, scribble suggestions, ideas, creative outputs, which are then collected. The result is pretty consistent.

The group who are told to come up with lots of ideas, do. But many, if not all of their ideas, are also the same as others in their group. There are lots of different uses for bricks, but they are the same alternative uses that everyone else is coming up with. Now the surprise. The people who are told to *Be Creative* come up with far *fewer* ideas for alternative uses for a brick, but those few ideas are far more likely to be completely unique within the classroom full of creative brains. And if the groups are swapped and the *Be Creative* people are told to 'come up with lots' and the 'come up with lots' group are told to *Be Creative,* the same thing happens. It seems that something occurs within us when we are told to *Be Creative*, and we do. We are able to engage a deeper level of consideration and thought to create less, but more unique, more divergent, creative solutions. The only thing that has changed is being told *'Be Creative.'* Or telling yourself to *Be Creative.* Imagine how powerful that is? What if a short person could tell themselves; 'Just be taller'? And they are. Whilst it may feel like we aren't creative, or maybe we have had our creative passions squashed and so have left them to dry out, the solution is, on face value, very simple. Just tell yourself, *Be Creative.* It's a brilliant start, but nothing is ever as simple as it looks. That's what we're going to play with throughout this book, but you need to have that basic, fundamental understanding. You *are* creative. But what does that *mean*? What is actually happening? Perhaps being creative is not as simple as it looks.

Let's have a look at another experiment that explores *The Be Creative Effect.* This one is called the *Divergent Associations Task,* so it can have the TLA of DAT. It was first suggested in

2021 by Jay Olsen and colleagues, so this one is new and exciting. And in colour. But before we get to that, I need to throw in a fairly useful little observation about creativity in the real world and how we use it.

There are books and papers everywhere all about Problem Solving Creativity (Or PSC if you prefer.) From people like Edward de Bono, famous for the concept of 'lateral thinking' or Johan Hoorn, whose *Creative Confluence* makes the point that 'Problem solving and, subsequently, decision making are traditionally seen as goal-driven activities.' (68) Most creativity discussion leans toward this one particular *type* of creativity: Problem Solving Creativity. This is creativity that is guided, used, or focused on problem solving. I mean, it's written on the box right? No explanation needed. Problem Solving Creativity is how Einstein worked out that $E=mc^2$. It's how Agatha Christie helped us work out 'Whodunit', it's how John Lennon took a nice phrase and turned it into a classic song. It's also how we all sit in the classroom and work out what to do with that brick. In each case there is a 'problem' to be solved. And the creative machine that is a human being drives on in some strange and mystical way until 'Pop', out comes a solution. Yes, there's a lot more to it than that, otherwise this book would be short and useless, but the general principle is pretty easy to grasp right? If there is a problem and it needs solving and you are told, or tell yourself, to 'Be Creative' and solve this problem, then that is Problem Solving Creativity.

Good. Right. Got it.

Problem Solving Creativity is shared by teachers, advertising executives and books aimed at people wanting to wear suits and have long business lunches. It is also scientific creativity, it is the creative business thinking, the start-up, the new business, making the better mousetrap, all that sort of creativity. As such it can be seen to be very much 'in the box' and is why people talk of creativity as breaking out of the box. There's more about 'the box' on page 179 but for now, for creative problem solving, let's assume the box is important. The box means that, mostly, the creativity is aimed at a specific outcome. Such as; make the company more profitable; get more clients; sell more products; explain gravity or viral infection. Building a better mousetrap requires creativity that is constrained. There is a box. For a start, you're all about killing mice. Or at least capturing them. Also you are preceded by things like history; this mouse trap is better *than* something. There is price, ease of use and attractiveness to shape the final outcome. But mostly, for creative problem solving, the very beginning of the process is directed toward a specific outcome. We have a problem that must be solved. The end begins the process. This type of thinking can be described as 'convergent' as it comes to a point. It converges where it is required.

This is fundamentally different to the other creativity. What I'm going to call Untethered Creativity. What might be seen as the artistic kind of creativity. This is often problem solving as well, such as a novelist working out how the butler did it. But that comes *after* the free ranging, unfocused, untethered creativity. This is the creativity that says 'Imagine a story where *this* happens...' or 'This riff in my head...' or 'Birds are cool. I wish I was a bird.' This is the note pad by my bed. The idle mind that drifteth like a cloud. It can also be labelled 'Divergent' thinking. Ideas and concepts that go... wherever. It is divergent creativity that ISN'T trying to solve a problem.

This is the Untethered Creativity. It is the flash and spark of inspiration that, as yet, has no outcome. Perhaps it has, as yet, no 'value.' It is simply a great idea that popped into your head. The problem with this idea is that the Untethered Creativity is very hard to spot because as soon at the inspiration hits us, we will shuffle it into some form of context. It begins to be worked on and 'solved'. If a unique, startling lyric appears in *my* head, I'll want to write a story around it. If the same lyric appeared in John Lennon's head, he would have put it in a song. If the same lyric popped into the head of Salvador Dali, a picture might be created. The Problem Solving Creativity would pick up the Untethered Creativity and give it 'value'. Or purpose. Or direction. It would make the divergent, convergent.

At the initial stage, however, this untethered creative thought has no box. There is no defined, targeted, creative product attached to the untethered creative thinking. This idea can become a novel, a mechanical device, a short story, movie, tattoo, wall art, social media post, a theory of world peace, anything. But to begin with, it's just an idea that has struck you. Often at the most inappropriate or inconvenient time. It is just an idea that hasn't yet been wrestled into any useful form. It is the kind of creative idea John Cleese might consider being 'Original thought' but has yet to move into Sir Ken Robinson's definition of 'Having value'. There has yet to be 'Process.' It makes sense, then, that Problem Solving Creativity and Untethered Creativity need each other.

Most highly effective creative people will be able to throw their idea across many forms or 'values', but the process of creativity can begin untethered from the 'value', time or even a reason. The skilled creative can begin, for example, writing a short story about sheep and end up with a magazine article about cardigan fashion, flowing wherever the story may take them. The untethered creative thinker can be having dinner with their partner and suddenly have a killer idea for an energy saving device. And then have to apologise to their partner for leaping out of the room during their romantic date night. The untethered creative thought has no bounds, no demands and, frequently, very bad timing. The other side of creativity, the Problem Solving Creativity, cannot survive like that. The creative problem solver does not want to look for a better mouse trap and end up with a unique haloumi recipe. However, the mouse trap will come from the same well of creativity as the untethered song lyric or the poetic turn of phrase. And, once the untethered creative idea is captured, it will require the creative problem solving to turn it into a creation with value. It will require process. That will require domain excellence, being good at what you do. More on that later, but for now, let's clear away one common confusion that appears when you don't understand what your creativity is trying to do. Ask yourself this:

Do I want to create for a specific end? Am I operating as a creative problem solver? You will say yes if you are doing things like creating a product, a service or a message for a particular purpose. If you are in the recording studio trying to turn that crazy song lyric into a hit tune. Or you are trying to establish Whodunit? Or why? If you are expanding on the creative idea you had and turning it into a creation, you are problem solving.

Into all of this, to make things a little more complicated, will come questions like; why do I want to create this? What do I want my song, book, tattoo, t-shirt design, light bulb, mousetrap etc. to bring to the world? What do I want to achieve with this? What is its value? These are questions we rarely ask but, as we shall soon see, these motivations are deeply fundamental to what and why you are reading this.

For the moment let's just accept that these questions will fall into the realm of your domain excellence. In a nutshell this means that the better you get at what you do, the better you will be at executing your Creative Problem Solving. And your creative problem solving will be used to fashion your Untethered

Creative idea and turn it into a creation of value. Whew. Got that?

Now we can have another look at these *'Be Creative'* experiments and the newer version called the Divergent Associations Task. (Yep, the DAT.)

Again, a potted version, for those of who don't want to read haemorrhoid inducing piles of academic explanation:

The Divergent Associations Task is kind of like saying 'Think about something you're not thinking about.' Participants are asked to write down ten nouns, ten words for things, in a list. The only stipulation is that none of these words can be associated with any other word on the list. Try it. It's pretty tricky! Especially when you then go through and take out three words that *might* have an association. So, for example, if CAT is one of your words, FIRE HOSE may not seem associated, unless you have an allergy, and cats make your eyes burn. The people at Harvard University who developed the DAT have a computer program that trawled billions of websites looking for 'common' associations in order to confirm the divergence of the words. The experimental results suggest that anyone can do this and create a list of very divergent words. This is important since one of the defining factors of creativity is that it diverges from the expected, it is 'original thought.' (It is what AI can NOT do.) By now you will have noticed the different 'types' of creativity involved here. The AUT, working out what to do with a brick, is focused on solving a problem. The DAT, making words that don't connect in any way, is the opposite. It is untethered and demands that you *don't* connect the dots.

So what we can see is that Problem Solving Creativity differs from Untethered Creativity. So What? Why does it matter to make this definition?

In her book about *The Creative Mind,* Margaret Boden defines two outcomes for creativity. Once it has 'been completed,' (a very questionable statement in itself) what 'type' of creativity is created? She points to H-Creativity and P-Creativity. Two 'outcomes,' or types of creativity. (32) H-Creativity has a historic result: The double helix explanation of DNA, The Mona Lisa, Eine Kline Nachtmusik, Velcro, Thomas the Tank engine, the beehive hairdo. All of these can be seen as H-Creative. Creative outputs that have had an historical impact. (I was going to mention the song "Baby Shark" here, but no-one wants that earworm.)

The P-Creative refers to psychological creativity (which is confusing) or Personal Creativity, which makes a lot more sense. P-Creativity is what we do all the time and often don't even recognise we are doing it. The creative work going on in your head. Should I wear that tie? With those shoes? The roses should be planted there. I think for dinner tonight I'll make... P-Creative is the creative choices we make every day. Any act of bringing something into existence that a person does will likely include P-Creativity. But that creative act is unlikely to have a historical impact. Your decision to wear that scarf with those pants won't shake the world to its foundations. Probably. Perhaps I'll make a letterbox that looks like a battleship. That's P-Creativity. Until it becomes a fad, then a trend, then an accepted norm. When every home has a letterbox like a battleship, then, maybe it can be considered H-Creative. But you don't get to decide when your creation is historically creative.

Let's go back to the *'Be Creative'* experiments. These showed that pretty much everyone and anyone can create and be a creative thinker. But no one is going to pick up your list of ten divergent words and say 'Well, this is going to change the world'. They are P-Creative. And they are untethered. However, it is conceivable that by problem solving the uses for a brick, a new paradigm for our lives may emerge. An H-Creative outcome. Maybe aerated concrete was invented this way? Who knows?

The point is, creativity is everywhere and always, but knowing what *type* of creativity is required for a particular purpose can be very useful.

Those people with the sparkling teeth and expensive suits who stand in the corporate meeting room and tell you to 'be creative, throw your ideas in', they make one mistake. Other than their decision to wear too much aftershave. They tell you that

'There's no such thing as a bad idea.' That's not true. Throwing a match at a man soaked in after shave is a bad idea. What they really mean is 'Don't just try to come up with *lots* of ideas, aim for *unique* ideas. And right there, what they are trying to do is get your brain to Untether and solve a problem. But if we recognise that these can be two different processes, we see that flaming aftershave man is asking us to do something we're not designed for.

Some good creative ideas can come from these sessions; what one company I know calls 'Blue Sky Sessions.' But this is because the individuals being crammed into this creative straight jacket are actually really good at thinking in these constrictive places anyway. It's the individual minds that make these things work, the P-Creative, not the meetings themselves. (At the company where I worked, 'Blue Sky Sessions' were always diarised as 'BS Sessions'. Just putting that out there.)

This leads me to that third way of understanding our creative output. Gregory Feist calls it Pro-C Creative, meaning 'Professional Creativity.' Not quite historically relevant H-creativity, but more than just 'something I came up with' Personal P-Creativity. Between them may lie the great wealth of what we call creative output. Since calling it 'pro-creative' is going to get really confusing, I'm opting for 'Effective Creativity'. Let's call it E-Creativity. P-Creativity plus process. Bear with me, this is worth it...

E-Creativity, Effective Creativity, is the creativity that leads to a creation or created product that does what it was designed to do and does it well. It solves a problem and gets on with just being. For example, I have written many published, award-winning stories, I have written and broadcast hundreds of comedy sketches on TV and Radio. My stories have not attained the H-Creative fame of Charles Dickens' work. None of my sketches have reached the H-Creative peaks of Monty Python's Parrot sketch or John Cleese's silly walk. And yet each of my pieces has done its job, in its place, at the time. It was effective. Someday, maybe, some of it will attain the status of H-Creativity, but for now, I can strive for Effective Creativity.

If you're trying to invent a better mousetrap, that bizarre dream last night about singing golf balls is going to be totally useless. If you want to write a fun song for kids, forget about brainstorming how to trap rodents and go with that golf ball thing. The *reason* for the creative output, the effectiveness of the creative product, needs to be considered. And this is where we lean on the E-Creative. Effective Creativity is where you grab hold of your P-Creative, your personal, individual unique inspirations, those late-night notes, flashes and bolts out of the blue, and put them to work.

E-Creativity is the *process* of creating, drawing from your creative well, of going from creative idea to created product. When I say product, I'm not referring to just commercial products like songs, novels, mousetraps, car commercials, etc.

etc. The product output of E-Creativity is everything. Your garden, that cake, the way you plate up dinner, the actual cooking of dinner, the way you play sport. Interestingly, whatever you make using your Effective Creative powers will, probably, come from a lot of P-Creativity. Those little flashes of ideas and uniqueness that help the whole thing emerge. For example, if you're cooking an omelette, P-Creative may suggest throwing in fresh basil. The E-Creative process will determine when and how much. When in the studio producing that song, the flash of P-Creative inspiration will say 'This needs a cello'. Then the E-Creative will work out how to effectively make that work in a song about singing golf balls.

So, Creativity comes in a lot of different shapes, for a lot of different purposes. When you mix them up and use the 'wrong' type at the 'wrong' time, you can feel you are not creative at all, or you are weird, or you just don't fit in.

Finally, we come back to the central definition of the creative process. Creativity leads to a product. This is the 'it has value' part of the definition. But it comes from inspiration, a unique idea or thought. P-Creative. That is the 'original idea' part of the definition. But the thing missing from all of this, the thing that makes creativity into creation, the thing that makes us all bend or break, stumble and get up again, is… Work. The E-Creative. The process.

And that brings us to the end of this brief look at what Creativity is. Shortly we'll pick this apart a bit more and play with some ways to work your creativity and make it more effective. From here we're going to dive into all the things that can go right and wrong as we turn little creative ideas into big creative outcomes. How we go from P-Creative to E-Creative.

But what about H-creativity? How will I become Historically relevant? As mentioned earlier, you don't get to decide when your effective creativity becomes historically relevant. As Voltaire noted a few hundred years ago, 'It is with books as with men: a very small number play a great part.' (14) The problem for many people is that they are highly effective creatives, but they have been striving for historically powerful works. Maybe don't do that. It's not something you can determine. In fact, trying to achieve historical creativity may well be one of things killing so many creative people. As Rich Gold notes, 'It's impossible to tell the difference between a crackpot and a genius until vision succeeds.' (36) So don't sweat it. Let's just work out how to work it.

It All Boils Down To This:

Creativity. What it is or is it?

- Every single human being is creative. No matter what.
- The expression of creativity is unique to each individual, which can make it seem mysterious or unpredictable to others.
- Creativity is a process. Bringing a creation from your creativity takes time.
- Creativity has a number of different modes. Untethered or Problem Solving. Personal, Effective or Historical. Knowing which mode you need or are using is helpful to ensure you don't get tangled in your own creative process.
- Creation of a creative product draws on skills and experiences. These can be developed and grown to make the process more efficient. You CAN learn to be more creatively effective.

Angelou, Maya. *The Paris Review Interviews, IV.* 1990. Picador. 2009

Atwood, Margaret, in Jacobs, Ben and Hjalmarsson, Helena (eds) *The Quotable Book Lover*. Skyhorse publishing. 1999

Bayly, Stephen and Mavity, Roger. *How to steal fire.* Bantam. 2019

Bell, Genevieve. Revolution now. *Cosmos*. Vol 89. Pp 80-87. 2021

Boden, Margaret. *The Creative Mind*. Cardinal books. 1992

Christensen, P. R., Guilford, J. P., & Wilson, R. C. Relations of creative responses to working time and instructions. *Journal of Experimental Psychology,* Vol 53. *No* 2. Pp 82–88. 1957

Cleese, John. *Creativity*. Hutchinson. 2020

Crabtree, Jeff and Julia. *Living with a creative Mind.* Zebra Collective, 2011

Csikszentmihalyi, Mihaly. *Flow. The Psychology of optimal experience.* Harper Collins ebook. Retrieved December 3rd. 2021.

DeBono, Edward. *Lateral Thinking*. Penguin. 1991

Feist, G. J., Dostal, D., & Kwan, V. Psychopathology in World-Class Artistic and Scientific Creativity. *Psychology of Aesthetics, Creativity, and the Arts*. Oct 21. 2020

Gold, Rich. *The Plenitude: Creativity, Innovation, and Making Stuff*, The MIT Press. 2007

Hallaert, Jenelle M. Flow, Creativity, and Suicide Risk in College Art Majors, *Creativity Research Journal,* Vol 31. No 3. Pp 335-341. 2019

Hemingway, Ernest. *Ernest Hemingway: The last interview and other conversations.* Melville House. 2015

Hoorn, Johan F. *Creative Confluence.* John Benjamin publishing. 2014

Hudson, L. *Contrary imaginations: A psychological study of the English schoolboy.* New York, NY: Routledge Library Editions, Psychology of Education. (Originally published 1966). 1996

Kaufman, James C and Sexton, Janel D. Why Doesn't the Writing Cure Help Poets? *Review of General Psychology* Vol. 10. No. 3. Pp 268–282. 2006

Kladder, Jonathan and William, Lee. Music Teachers Perceptions of Creativity: A Preliminary Investigation, *Creativity Research Journal.* Vol 31. No 4. Pp 395-407. 2019

London, Joan. *The Writer's Room.* Wood, Charlotte (ed) Allen and Unwin. 2016

Mammadov, Sakhavat. In Search of Temperament and Personality Predictors of Creativity: A Test of a Mediation Model. *Creativity Research journal.* Vol 31. No 2. Pp 174–187. 2019

McLeish, Tom. Creativity, imagination and being in the image of God: a Précis of The Poetry and Music of Science. *Interdisciplinary Science Reviews.* Vol. 45. No 1 Pp 1–7. 2020

Murakami, Hyuki. *The Paris Review Interviews, IV.* Picador. 2009

Olsen, Jay, et al. Naming unrelated words predicts creativity. *PNAS 2021.* Vol 118. No 25. https://doi.org/10.1073/pnas.2022340118 Retrieved 09/2021

Pao, Derick. Foreword in *Creativity: When East Meets West.* Sing Lau, et al (eds.) World Scientific. 2004

Renzulli, Joseph s. The three-ring conception of giftedness: A developmental model for creative productivity. In *Conceptions of Giftedness 2nd ed.* Sternberg, R.J and Davidson, J.E. (eds) Cambridge University Press New York pp 246- 279. 1986

Robinson, Ken. *Can Creativity be Taught*? https://www.youtube.com/watch?v=vlBpDggX3iE Retrieved 03/2020

Somerset Maugham, William. *The Quotable Book Lover*. Jacobs, Ben and Hjalmarsson, Helena (eds) Skyhorse publishing. 1999

Voltaire. *The Quotable Book Lover*. Jacobs, Ben and Hjalmarsson, Helena (eds) Skyhorse publishing. 1999

Walia, Chetan. A Dynamic Definition of Creativity, *Creativity Research Journal,* Vol 31 No 3. Pp 237-247. 2019

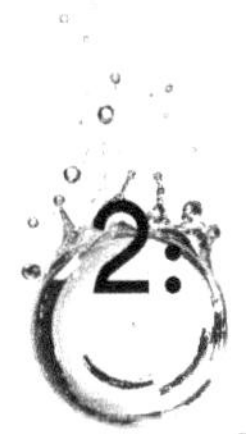

2: How have we got it so wrong?

> The key question isn't "What fosters creativity?" But it is why in God's name isn't everyone creative? Where was the human potential lost? How was it crippled?
>
> ABRAHAM MASLOW

We've had a dig into what decades of science and research thinks creativity is and wrestled with the fact that it may be hard to define and may come in all sorts of different types and, for different reasons, may address different uses. So, yes, there's a lot of confusion and a lot of variation. This is why a book on Distilling Creativity can't just say 'Do this, don't do that,' because for you, doing 'that' might be perfect. Or problematic. But what happens when we look at what a creative person is like? Are there things that are common? Let's look at some folks who are obviously involved in creative work.

Joan London is an author. She says,

> …by the nature of their work [writers] are cut off from others, sitting long hours alone in a room. They are outsiders because of the risk they take—every book is a risk. Because of their vulnerability, exposing their inner worlds. (249)

Jack Kerouac is a writer who also came to be part of the shape and sound of the culture of 60's America. He said that 'writing at least is a silent meditation even though you're going a hundred miles an hour.' (104) EB White, who brought us *Charlotte's Web*, points out that 'in the end a man must sit down and get the words on paper, and against great odds. This takes stamina and resolution.' (155) We could go on and on with famous and not so famous writers pointing to the solitary pursuit that is writing creatively. Sometimes, musicians will feel it too. Pop star Amy Shark told *Rolling Stone* magazine that her music career became more focused when, 'I started realising I didn't need anybody… That it is in me, it's all up to me to write the album… A good song's a good song and that's in me. I'm in control of that. That's my job.' (Reid, 33) When John McDonald interviewed Australian painters about their creative process, he introduced his book by saying that,

> Every painter has a touch of narcissism, maybe a trace of megalomania. To work long hours in solitude requires a strong belief in the value of one's vision… The artist

> who is lonely in the studio is probably in the wrong profession. (11)

Among the painters he spoke with, Guo Jian confessed that '... Lots of times I sit in front of a half-painted canvas, and I can't do anything. I'll spend the whole day just sitting there but nothing comes.' (78) Yvette Watt also highlighted the solitary nature of her work. 'I have this imaginary audience in my head as I'm working. It is a neurosis of sorts, but I think that's inevitable because it's such a solitary thing that you do.' (242)

If you're wanting to understand creativity, this is a hugely important point. The act of writing and of painting *is* a solitary act. No one else can do it for you. The English satirist and screen writer Georgia Pritchet in her book *My Mess is a Bit of a Life*, says that, 'Writing is the perfect job for an anxious person. You get to do most of it at home in your pyjamas. It is utterly anonymous. Nobody knows what writers look like.' (127) And therein lies the problem for the understanding of creativity. Is it being highly creative that makes creative writers' loners, or is it the act of writing or painting itself? See the difference? Perhaps if Georgia Pritchet was a highly skilled flautist, rather than a writer, she would find her creativity reaching its peak when surrounded by the rest of the orchestra. For the flautist Georgia, creativity may become a communal, group pursuit. Or if Jack Kerouac had become a skilled football coach, perhaps he would not be creating at a hundred miles an hour by himself, but rather as part of a unified team. As a movie director, perhaps Yvette Watt would find that the collaborative process of movie making would alleviate some of her neurosis?

Creating *can* be a solitary process, but that does not mean that creativity *needs* isolation. Is it *necessarily* a solo process? No. Many performers, artists and creators, work in tight and effective collaboration. The very nature of certain creative products demands relationships of creativity. Far from sitting alone in their room, a movie director, a radio announcer, an actor, a stand-up comic, a make-up artist... you get the idea; in most creative industries in fact, the process of creativity is done in groups or partnerships. Music legend Eric Clapton sums up his understanding nicely;

> I never play alone. I very rarely play alone at home, or in a hotel room, or anywhere. I very rarely travel with a guitar. I tend to keep all of that bottled up, until there's an audience to play to. I think music is a shared experience.... It's like it gains value according to the certain circumstances. (531)

Tammy Wynette, a country performer of an earlier generation, makes a really interesting point. She said, 'I think I have more confidence in something I've done with somebody else, I don't know why.' (278)

In fact, there is probably a whole line in creativity here that applies only in groups. It's worth noting. It's what Laura Bishop highlights as 'emergence', an aspect of creativity that happens when the wonderful and unique connections that define creative convergence, are coming from a number of brains, all working toward a similar creative outcome. She points out that:

> ... emergence occurs when a group performs in a way that cannot be attributed to any one individual contributor. (3)

Her research goes on to note that:

> In performing creatively, ensemble musicians face two primary challenges: generating original (but stylistically appropriate) ideas and maintaining coordination While translating these ideas into musical output. (4)

For these groups, performing is an intense nexus of the free-flowing creativity and, at the same time, the tight focused understanding of the outcome, the product. It's a fascinating way of considering creativity, that a group becomes the creative 'individual,' and each member is only as good as their ability to be both convergent and divergent at the same time. It's also a consideration that can be seen, in some way, in pretty much any group creative environment. Actors on stage, or with a director, radio teams, choirs, engineers in a meeting, chefs in the kitchen, authors and their editors. Some people always work creatively in these groups. In fact, it is pretty much just the writers who deliberately and constantly go it alone. And the painters. Thus, there has emerged a mythology that this is because of the way their creativity works. But maybe it's not. Creating is not necessarily an individual pursuit. Writing or painting, however, is. Obviously, this has repercussions for those of us who write or paint, but for now we're unpacking what is the underlying structure of creativity, not just the nature of writing or painting.

Yes... and No

George Young, who wrote many of the anthems of Australian rock, is quick to debunk the 'mystery' of songwriting.

> I've heard a lot of psychobabble about this down through the years, some of it vaguely plausible. But in general terms, I don't believe there is any mystery. Songs come from using your imagination and drawing on your own experience of life. (75)

Well, that's nice. Simple. To the point. But it directly contradicts Iva Davies, who wrote another of Australia's rock anthems, *Great Southern Land*. He says that,

> 'I still don't understand the process. I haven't got any better at making that big leap, because, for me, it's really hard. It's never become any easier.' Because it's a mysterious process? he was asked. 'Yes.' (390)

This perfectly describes the problem with understanding your own creativity. Contradiction.

Every single person will create in their own way, will understand it differently and find different issues and triggers. For some it will be a mystery, for others it will simply be a logical process. Some will feverishly slog away and find they have created nothing. Others will dream a classic overnight. The biggest contradiction is that the same individual may do all of these things at different times. But fear not, there are certain aspects of the creative life that are consistent, regular and knowable. By understanding these 'knowables' we may be able to more effectively understand our own contradictory creativity. So, let's go back to the laboratory and see what science has come up with.

What's the answer when we ask; 'What type of person is a creative person'? What does every highly effective individual have in common? Are they all extroverts or introverts? Are they all highly focused, or are they distracted dreamers? Are they outgoing or do they hide from attention?

The answer is simple.

Yes.

And No.

What we are looking at is not an exclusive dichotomy, either one or the other, but a composite. What the business suits might call a synergy. What they mean is ‘Why can’t it be both?’

It can be said that many highly effective creative people are seen as confident, outgoing, loud even. Or possibly quite tetchy, maybe arrogant, even rude. But keep in mind that these are complete human beings, and we see only their public presence. We could get into a whole conversation about how, when we are in public, everyone ‘performs’ who they are, and thus, when you are in public because of your creativity, which is something you are very good at or passionate about, you perform as that person. It may be why sports people are often seen as a bit thick. All they talk about is football, or golf, or whatever they play. But that’s because that’s all the media ever ask them about, and it’s what they have spent a very committed, full-on life perfecting. If you asked them about parenting or cooking or their favourite dog, you might suddenly find a totally different person. But it's not. It’s the same person, we just see them differently. So, the thing to note; all these ideas that ‘creative people are like that’ or ‘rock stars are drugged-out slackers’ or ‘all poets are neurotic loners’ or ‘all scientists are scatterbrained obsessives’ or ‘all writers are addle-headed dreamers,’ may simply be a misattribution born of generations of looking in from the outside and assuming we see the whole truth.

It is also worth noting that if someone has a little bit of weirdness, that will become the focus of the world. Like Einstein's crazy hair. But don't we all have a little bit of weirdness? Therefore, some of the creative stereotypes are born of a certain statistical bias, but if you want to be an effective creative individual, you can't live the stereotype. Why not? Because it's not *you*. It's a fiction, a figment of a cultural imagination. These things that we see from the outside are rarely what they seem. Perhaps the only common factor among all highly creative types is that they have a pulse. Sometimes it rushes, sometimes it is relaxed, but they are alive.

(By 'highly creative types' I simply mean those individuals who have chosen a pursuit that makes their creativity visible to the wider world. As already stated, everyone is creative, it is simply a matter of how much and how efficiently we engage with it and how the rest of the world allows us to do so.)

It is worth looking at what are the personality factors more *likely* to be present in someone who is in that publicly, or even the historically, H-creative, group. The famous ones, those who have gone before. Therefore, I want to bring in a problematic but helpful thing.

The Big 5 Personality traits.

In the 1930's Gordon Allport and Henry Odbert began trying to quantify human personality. (I can't help thinking there was a personal investment from a guy named 'Odbert'.) Then in 1949, in the shadow of world wars and global conflict, at a time when psychology was trying to emerge as a force, and when people were starting to realise we needed to understand ourselves better, there came the idea of the Big 5 personality traits. This work was led by a chap called D.W. Fiske. The idea was that there are five areas of personality, or traits, and people are all living their lives somewhere in these five areas. With these traits in mind, is it possible to identify who is highly creative and who is not?

Yes.

And no.

Let me walk you through the traits, because I know you want to see where *you*, personally sit. And then we'll look at why the traits can be traitorous.

The Big 5 personality Traits, laymen's version:

Openness:

As it sounds, being open. You rate high in Openness if you are open to experiences, new things, new tastes, new adventures. This correlates with expanded imagination and insights. We'll dig into this later, but for now, the science says that greater openness leads to more comfort with ambiguity and allows for greater lateral thinking. You rate high in openness if you're the first to eat the witchetty grub and the last to order 'the usual.' When they say, 'You can't do that', it is taken as a challenge rather than an instruction.

Low Openness is expressed as a traditional view, love of the comfort zone and not a lot of problem solving.

Conscientiousness:

A high rating on this trait suggests you are thoughtful, have good impulse control, and you can focus effectively on goal directed behaviours. This is the trait of the details person. They hear 'You can't do that' and begin to enumerate the factors that might suggest this. Conscientiousness means you plan ahead, even whilst in the here and now. They are the person who will say 'We should do this again sometime,' and already have their diary out. The person low in conscientiousness won't even have a diary, dislikes structure and has turned procrastination into a lifestyle.

Extroversion:

This one is a little confusing because it's not about being loud or obnoxious, it refers to people who get energised when in the company of others. They come alive. Comedian Mike Myers refers to himself as 'a site-specific extrovert', since he will be at rest, withdrawn even, when alone, but put him onstage and the extrovert emerges. Robin Williams agreed wholeheartedly with this description of himself too. A blazing human connection machine, complete flow when on stage, but also happy to be in a country where no one knows him and he can be alone (Williams). Many performers would fit this 'site specific' version of extroversion. For the Big 5 trait analyses, if someone says, 'How are you doing?' and you can roll out a twenty-minute PowerPoint presentation, you're probably rating high on extroversion. The person low in extroversion will favour a shrug and a 'whatever,' and go back to the corner they prefer.

Agreeableness:

When you tell the highly agreeable individual 'You can't do that' they will likely agree wholeheartedly, seeing the problems it may cause for others. However, if the rest of the group decide to do it anyway, the agreeable individual will, according to the trait, join in whole-heartedly. They are the very picture of trust and kindness and probably rather altruistic. They are likely to help other people. They are likely to be volunteering, helping, or at least wanting to. They might be charity collectors. Those low in agreeableness are the ones who slam the door in the face of charity collectors. They are, as my mother would say, 'disagreeable' types.

Neuroticism:

Not to be confused with eroticism. In fact, it's *really* different. Being high on the neurotic trait is a personification of sadness, grey clouds hover over them and they tend toward emotional instability. They are big on mood swings and anxiety and not so big on confidence and stability. They don't need someone to say 'You can't do this' as they are already quite convinced. It is important to note that this is a trait on its own and is not simply the opposite of the other, more 'positive' traits.

Those are some of the more established things that psychology holds up as foundational to human personality. According to the logic of the Big 5, each one of us is on a sliding scale on each of these traits and this will determine the 'type' of person we are. Over the generations, various other personality scales have been proposed, some as small as a couple of traits or as broad as four thousand. Perhaps to save arguments, it has become a consistent five factors. But the to-ing and fro-ing over the research and the meaning of it points to the big problem in all of this. This understanding is made to help organisations like armies and schools and factories work out what type of person will be best suited to being a grunt soldier, or a gifted student, or a process labourer and so on. In other words, this stuff is really good at helping to understand people. But it is really bad at helping you understand a person. It can give a general population average, but it doesn't really help you, as an individual. An artist like Nick Cave, who seems to be rather open, also may find himself rating high in neuroticism, such as when he observes that,

> If I can sit down and write a line, then put another one next to it and it rhymes beautifully… and it can be deeply sad, it can make me happier than anything. (434)

Deeply sad and very happy at the very same time.

Before we throw all this out as unhelpful corporate controlling, it's important to note that there is one quite robust finding from all of the research over the years. Darya Zabelina, in a paper looking at *Creative Achievement and Individual Difference*, states that,

> the link between openness/intellect and creativity is the most robust finding… this positive relationship is unsurprising given that creative people tend to be intellectually curious, imaginative, open-minded, and aesthetically sensitive … as all of these traits are

> expressed by people who score highly in openness to experience. (2)

Openness seems to be a major and consistent factor in the lives of creative people. Brian Grazer, the Hollywood producer behind movies like *Splash*, *Apollo 13*, *A Beautiful Mind* and many more, has even written a book exploring his own curiosity, his openness to new things, and how it fuels his life. In it he states, 'Curiosity has, quite literally, been the key to my success, and also the key to my happiness.' (xii)

The natural curiosity and openness to new experiences is stated consistently. Being open and curious is vital. In fact, it will feature shortly in a chapter all of its own. But what about the other four domains? Zabelina's paper went on to note that,

> Low agreeableness is also generally associated with creative achievement. For instance, young adults who score highly in agreeableness have fewer creative achievements in both genders... Similarly, within the scientific community (e.g., physicists, chemists, and biologists), low agreeableness predicts creative eminence... and artists score lower on agreeableness measures than do non artists. (2)

What this might suggest is that people who score low on agreeableness, who won't just go along with the crowd, do so from a desire to do something different. This may be because they see a sparkling new way of being, or because they are grumpy, or they just like being argumentative. Either way they are being low in agreeableness. This is another little thread of confusion when it comes to understanding creativity. How often do our most creative children and youths end up being creatively stifled because they are also being disagreeable? We'll open that can of worms later because it's a very important thing for anyone responsible for young minds, like teachers or parents. Or people in general.

Other work on the Big 5 personality traits suggests that, 'In particular the traits of risk taking, openness, individuality, perseverance and tolerance of ambiguity seem to play a role' (Lubart, 29). Patrick Bateson and his colleagues added that,

> creative people tend to be more open to new experiences, less conventional, less conscientious and more impulsive than less creative people. These characteristics are linked to relatively stable features of personality. (92)

And on and on it goes, with this Big 5 thing being applied to swathes of people over time. But what does it say about the individual, unique, you? Probably something like this:

Being open to new things, being curious, being experimental is pretty much the only consistent thing about creative people...

and even that, as we shall see, is not a thing you *are*, but something you can really learn and cultivate. Also, creative folks may not be so 'agreeable' but rather are willing to stand out, stand apart. The question that this collection of traits doesn't answer is this: Are highly creative people open to new things, or does the decision to be a creative force *make* you more open to new things? As we shall see the answer is;

Yes…

and No.

A word about…
The Gardener you choose to be.

I don't have a garden. I don't have veggies growing and my wife won't let me touch the indoor plants. Plants only come to me when they want to die. At best, I am voluntary assisted dying for vegetation. BUT, as a person who reads the bible, I know I am called to be a gardener. God created the world and put us all in it as his gardeners. And that means me too. Proving that God has a sense of humour. Fortunately, 'man as gardener' is a metaphor of sorts, otherwise creation is in big trouble. This all came to a head one holiday when my wife and I stayed in a place called Montville in Queensland. It is a thick, luscious rainforest. As we sat looking out at this wall of uncontrolled green growth, being eaten by mosquitos, pointing at cane toads and stopping the kookaburras from eating our breakfast, the peace was amazing. Also, there was no internet. Just this amazing rainforest. And the thought struck me. What am I supposed to DO with THIS garden as a gardener? Maybe it should ACTUALLY look like a perfectly manicured English estate? Trimmed lawn, neat edges, everything where I want it to be? And this is where the whole thing began to change my life. As a gardener in this creation, am I called to garden a wild, untamed, raucously verdant uncontrolled rainforest? Or am I meant to control and corner, edge and trim to make a perfect structured garden of immense correctness? Which of these gardens is God wanting me to work with? And that then raises questions like this:

Do I let my thoughts, my dreams, my children, my work, run wild? Like a rainforest? Or do I mow, trim and edge my thoughts, dreams, etc. to create an ordered English country estate? And who does the actual work? Humans shape the English garden, but not the rainforest so much. Are we working too hard to shape the garden, to guide and control our work, to a human design, or should we let it go more? Because the outcomes are vastly different. How many species of insect, mammal and plant flourish in a rainforest of rampant, uncontrolled growth? Apparently the Amazon is home to around 40,000 plant species, nearly 1,300 bird species, 3,000 types of fish, 427 species of mammals, and 2.5 million different insects… give or take.

And in an English country Garden? How many species exist? I'm guessing 235 precisely. Depending on the season. Notice in an English country garden, one is constantly fighting weeds and pests. In a rainforest there are no weeds and pests, just living things. Weeds and pests are something *we* decide on.

The point is that if I let 'nature' grow the garden, tend the garden, decide on the shape and makeup of the garden, anything can happen. Everything has a chance to flourish.

In a controlled and managed garden, there can only be what my human mind and imagination will allow. A human mind fighting to impose its will where, maybe, it should just let go and enjoy.

What about Flow?

There's one more important area of psychology that makes understanding creativity really confusing. Let's sort this out because it makes a lot of heads explode and it doesn't need to.

The problem is that bipolar disorder, a rather nasty and quite frightening psychological condition, once known as manic depression, looks a lot like 'flow', a wonderful and exciting element of creative power.

Rather than embracing the place of flow in their creative life, many people fear it in case they are becoming mentally ill. Let me show you what I mean. Here is a definition of bipolar from Kay Redfield Jamison in her book that explores bipolar and creativity. It's called *Touched by The Fire,* and she notes that;

> during hypomania and mania, mood is generally
> elevated and expansive (or, not infrequently, paranoid

> and irritable); activity and energy levels are greatly increased; the need for sleep is decreased; speech is often rapid, excitable, and intrusive; and thinking is fast, moving quickly from topic to topic. Hypomanic or manic individuals usually have an inflated self-esteem, as well as a certainty of conviction about the correctness and importance of their ideas. (13) Manic and hypomanic thoughts are flighty and leap from topic to topic; in milder manic states the pattern of association between ideas is usually clear. (29)

Now, here is a description of 'Flow', From Mihaly Csikszentmihalyi,

> ...one acts with a deep but effortless involvement that removes from awareness the worries and frustrations of everyday life... enjoyable experiences allow people to exercise a sense of control over their actions... concern for the self disappears, yet paradoxically the sense of self emerges stronger after the flow experience is over... the sense of the duration of time is altered; hours pass by in minutes, and minutes can stretch out to seem like hours. (49)

Both the manic phase of bipolar and the experience of flow can look very similar. They are all-engaging. They provide a tightness of focus and intensity of concentration. They exhibit connections between thoughts that can seem illogical. They occur within the attention of the individual, that is to say they are an internal, mental experience. Time becomes 'forgotten' or at least seems to dilate.

From the outside and from the inside, bipolar and flow can look very similar. Here's how some famous creators explain it. Novelist and musician Nick Cave notes that;

> The whole thing with writing and making music is that when I'm in the moment with it, I feel like a different person, I feel like what I'm doing is the greatest thing not only that I have done but that has ever been done.... When I go off stage or when I finish a record and it gets sent back to me and I have it in my hands, it's very anticlimactic. I realise I'm just this guy like everybody else. (432)

Little River Band songwriter Graham Goble says that, 'I'm well aware that when I'm in the writing experience, I feel completely different than when I'm in a normal experience' (205-206). Novelist Charlotte Wood describes it like this.

> When I'm immersed in creative work, time expands and everything else drops away—the neediness and strain,

> the depletion and fragmentation that pervades so much of contemporary life. (18)

Just as the belief that only a certain type of person can be highly creative is a myth, so is the myth that being highly creative is a mental problem, that when you create you are 'suffering' something like bipolar disorder. The similarity between bipolar and highly engaged creative flow have long been recognised but also, have long been seen as problematic by some. Let's just put this to bed. We are going to have a look at a more helpful understanding of the bipolar-looking aspects of creativity shortly and we'll dive into flow a bit more too, but for now, let's make it clear. Being incredibly and emphatically involved in creating is *not* a mental disorder. It is not a bad thing to find yourself swept away in the flow, to find yourself carried off by your incredible brain. Creativity is *not* bipolar disorder. But, because it looks a bit like it, it is something people get concerned about.

To see how easily this gets misconstrued, revisit those quotes from just before. They can be seen as describing either someone who is crazy… or someone who is creating.

> when I'm in the moment with it, I feel like a different person, (Nick cave)

> I feel completely different than when I'm in a normal experience. (Goble, 205-206)

> When I'm immersed in creative work, time expands and everything else drops away (Woods)

Let me make this really clear. Bipolar disorder is real. It messes up lives and needs to be treated by professionals. Creativity and flow is *not* a disorder. It needs to be used and understood by *you* so you can have a fruitful creative life.

This last point goes back to something we mentioned earlier; that there are some famous folk who *do* live with bipolar disorder and this then becomes part of their story, a part that is easy for the rest of us to turn into mythology. But think about it this way. If a highly creative individual has cancer and, after being diagnosed, starts creating amazing work, is it because of the cancer? Well, Yes. And No. The change of internal understanding brought on by a terminal condition might well unleash their process, but it's not the cancer that is doing the creating. By the same token, bipolar disorder, or depression, or autism, or anything, can be a comorbidity that allows greater engagement at some level through manic activity but is it what makes this person creative? Probably not. Otherwise, every bipolar individual could be incredibly, successfully, creative. And that is just not the case. As we've already noted, the public perception of creative people can make this very confusing. Sometimes, even the scientists in the field don't help. In a very neat bit of research about magicians and creativity, Gil

Greengross and Paul Silva make this claim to suggest that creativity is a potential problem;

> ...there are plenty of examples [of mental illness] among other creative occupations. Some of the famous cases include comedians (Robin Williams and Sarah Silverman), poets (Sylvia Plath), writers (Virginia Woolf), painters (Van Gogh and Georgia O'Keeffe), singers (Brian Wilson and Billie Eilish) and scientists (Kurt Gödel and John Nash). (Greengross et al, 5)

The kind of blasé reference to creative folk who have lived with a mental illness is not helpful because we use it to make *that* the thing we know about these people. And that's just not fair. *Anybody* can have a mental illness, no matter what their profession or pursuit. And equally worth noting, there are hordes of singers, poets, comedians, scientists etc. who *don't* have a mental illness. It is a misfortune of perception, that creativity is so easily shackled to pictures of mental illness. The research doesn't support it. But it's a much more exciting story. Don't blindly believe it. Sylvia Plath, who suffered terribly from mental health issues, deliberately noted that her mental state was not the key to her poetic brilliance. She said, 'When you are insane, you are busy being insane – all the time... when I was crazy, that's all I was.' (5) She was a brilliant poet. And also sometimes seriously mentally ill. But never at the same time. Being afraid of your creativity is a terrible lie. And, as we'll see, being highly creative can actually support better mental health, not necessarily damage it.

The trick here is to use your understanding of all these creative things, like the Big 5, bipolar disorder, and so on, to find out how *you* work, what is *your* way of unleashing yourself. Safely, consistently, and joyfully. Because that will be like no-one else. In fact, Mihaly Csikszentmihalyi, the one who coined 'flow', makes it obvious that flow is not the same thing for everyone, it cannot be seen as the same for all. He says that,

> Because optimal experience [aka flow] depends on the ability to control what happens in consciousness moment by moment, each person has to achieve it on the basis of his own individual efforts and creativity. (5)

Personality traits, flow states, all the stuff going on in your head, will be unique to you and that means you need to get your head around your own head, and how it works. Charlotte Wood puts it like this:

> The paradox I've learned is this: every artist must protect and obey their own peculiar instincts—and, simultaneously, those very instincts must be constantly challenged and refreshed and developed. (26)

Those instincts will fit loosely with the global understandings of personality and psychology, but they won't fit perfectly. Imagine your creativity is a pair of pants. All pants are roughly the same shape, but if you don't get the right size, the right shape, the right fit, you are going to get some nasty rubbing, right where you don't want it. Let's work out what will shape your personal creative pants.

It All Boils Down to This:

How have we got it so wrong?

- Creating *can* be a solitary process, but that does not mean that creativity *needs* isolation. In fact, as we'll see later, effective and healthy creativity often needs a community.
- There is a whole pile of assumptions about our creativity that are just plain wrong. Wrong because we are individuals, not a population and wrong because what it looks and feels like is not, necessarily, what it is.
- The sometimes unsettling feelings of highly creative activity are not, necessarily 'abnormal'. They don't need to be avoided or cured, but they do need to be understood and controlled for.
- Who you are, your personality, won't determine if you are very creative, but it may shape *how* you are very creative.
- In chapter 3 we are going to have a look at a way of understanding the creative process that looks like bipolar but is a much better way of understanding what is happening to you.

Bateson, Patrick, and Martin, Paul. *Play, Playfulness, Creativity and Innovation*. Cambridge. 2013

Bishop, Laura. Collaborative Musical Creativity: How Ensembles Coordinate Spontaneity. In *Frontiers in Psychology*. Vol 9. Article 1285. 2018

Cave, Nick. *Songwriters speak. Conversations about creating music.* Krueger, Debbie (ed) Limelight Press. Pp 415-427. 2005

Clapton, Eric. *Looking to get Lost; adventures in music and writing.* Guralnick, Peter (ed). Little Brown. Pp511-539. 2020

Csikszentmihalyi, Mihalyi. *Flow; the Psychology of Optimal experience.* Harper Collins, 2008

Davies, Iva. *Songwriters speak. Conversations about creating music.* Krueger, Debbie (ed) Limelight Press. Pp 386-400. 2005

Goble, Graham. *Songwriters speak. Conversations about creating music.* Krueger, Debbie (ed) Limelight Press. Pp 202-214. 2005

Grazer, Brian and Fishman, Charles. *A curious Mind: The Secret to a Bigger Life.* Simon and Schuster. 2015

Greengross, Gil, Silvia, Paul J. and Crasson, Sara J. Psychotic and autistic traits among magicians and their relationship with creative beliefs. *BJPsych Open*. Vol 9. No 214. Pp 1–6. Cambridge University Press 2023

Jamison, Kay Redfield. *Touched With Fire. Manic Depressive illness and the artistic temperament.* Free press. 1993

Jian, Guo. *Studio: Australian painters on the nature of creativity.* McDonald, John (ed) R. Ian Lloyd Productions. Tower Books. 2007.

Kerouac, Jack. *Paris Review Interviews IV.* Rushdie, Salman (ed). Vol 43. 1968. Pp 96-143. 2009

London, Joan. *The Writer's Room Conversation about writing by Charlotte Wood,* Allen and Unwin. Pp 148-173. 2016

Lubart Todd I. and Georgsdottir, Asta. Creativity: Developmental and Cross-Cultural Issues. In *Creativity; when East meets West.* Sing Lau, et al. (Eds) World Scientific. 2004.

Maslow, Abraham. In Schroeder, Bernhard. *Simply Brilliant.* Amacom. 2016

McDonald, John. *Studio: Australian painters on the nature of creativity.* R. Ian Lloyd Productions. Tower Books. 2007.

Panero, Maria Eugenia. A Psychological Exploration of the Experience of Acting, *Creativity Research Journal*, Vol 31. No 4. Pp 428-442. 2019

Plath Sylvia. in Introduction. *Poets on Prozac. Mental illness, treatment and the creative process.* Richard M Berlin. Johns Hopkins University press. 2008

Pritchet, Georgia. *My mess is a bit of a life.* Faber. 2021

Shark, Amy. Unguarded and Addictive. Reid, Poppy (ed) *Rolling Stone* June-August. Pp30-33. 2021.

White, E.B. *Paris Review Interviews IV.* Rushdie, Salman (ed). Vol 90. 1983. Pp 144-217. Picador. 2009

Watt, Yvette. *Studio: Australian painters on the nature of creativity.* R. Ian Lloyd Productions. p 242. Tower Books. 2007

Williams, Robin. *Inside the actors Studio.* Dir: Jeff Wurtz, EP: James Lipton. Gryphon Entertainment, 2008

Wood, Charlotte. *The Luminous solution* Allen and Unwin. 2021

Wynette, Tammy. *Looking to get Lost; adventures in music and writing*. Guralnick, Peter (ed). Pp 268-285. Little Brown. 2020

Young, George. *Songwriters speak. Conversations about creating music*. Krueger, Debbie (ed) Limelight Press. Pp 55-75. 2005

Zabelina, D. L., Zaonegina, E., Revelle, W., & Condon, D. M. Creative Achievement and Individual Differences: Associations Across and Within the Domains of Creativity. *Psychology of Aesthetics, Creativity, and the Arts*. Oct 5. 2021

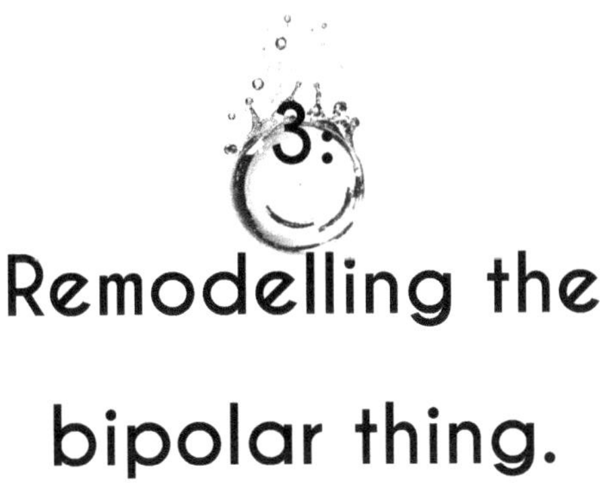

3: Remodelling the bipolar thing.

> Here, Jean Dubuffet's famous quote comes to mind: "there's no more an art of the insane than there is an art of dyspeptic people or the art of people with knee problems" (156)
>
> ERIK THUYS

Now we know what Creativity is and what it isn't. Sort of. We've established a definition and buried some of the most problematic myths and misbeliefs. The table is set. Let's get stuck in.

We noted earlier that bipolar disorder is often seen as a parallel for creativity, that it has been used as an analogue. But creativity isn't bipolar. So let's start there.

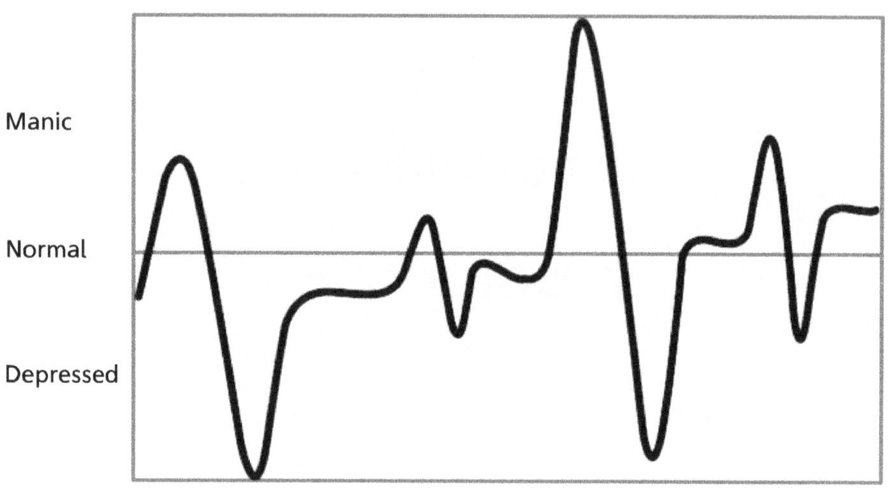

The traditional model of bipolar disorder looks like this, a sine wave of mood that drops to depression and then rises, through a state of 'normal' and then on into the manic phase, before sliding back down the hill, through a bout of 'normal' and on into the depressed phase. Okay, that's not a clinical description, but you get the idea. The various 'states' will vary in duration, intensity and clarity but, like we saw earlier, this is a general picture, not a specific individual presentation. Bipolar disorder sees the sufferer going up to hypomanic, crazy energy states, then 'normalising' before plummeting into varying depths of clinical depression.

That's a very layman version of bipolar.

And the fact is, much of the creative life mimics this kind of rollercoaster. Author E.L. Doctrow said that 'Writing is a socially acceptable form of schizophrenia' and V.S. Pritchett speaks of 'the depression and sense of nothingness that comes when a piece of work is done.' Maya Angelou says that,

> Some work flows and, you know, you can catch three days. I think the word in sailing is scudding—you know, three days of just scudding. Other days it's just awful—plodding and backing up, trying to take out all the ands, ifs, tos, fors, buts, wherefores, therefores, howevers—you know, all those. (271)

Painter Robin Wallace Crabbe is well aware of his own ups and downs. 'I do quite a lot of sitting around… there's a lot of just sitting around playing. Probably more sitting around playing than there is earnest protestant painting.' The list of artists who share this experience goes on and on. As Tim Finn puts it, his songwriting emerges from this constant swinging back and forth. 'Is anybody upbeat all the time? Songwriters allow themselves perhaps to feel it more. It's not sadness, it's just melancholy of things passing and changing.' (256)

As we saw in the previous chapter, being creative and being bipolar can look very similar.

But if you're someone who has experienced great flow, creative highs and times of intense creativity, you'll notice something very, astoundingly, wrong with the bipolar picture as an analogue for the creative life.

Think performers on a stage, in concerts, comedians, actors. Think sports people, footballers, tennis players. Think public speakers, preachers. In *all* of these cases you can clearly see them go through a very similar version of this bipolar model. But the difference is vital. For them, for us who do live an active, creative life, the model of our mood and engagement probably looks more like…

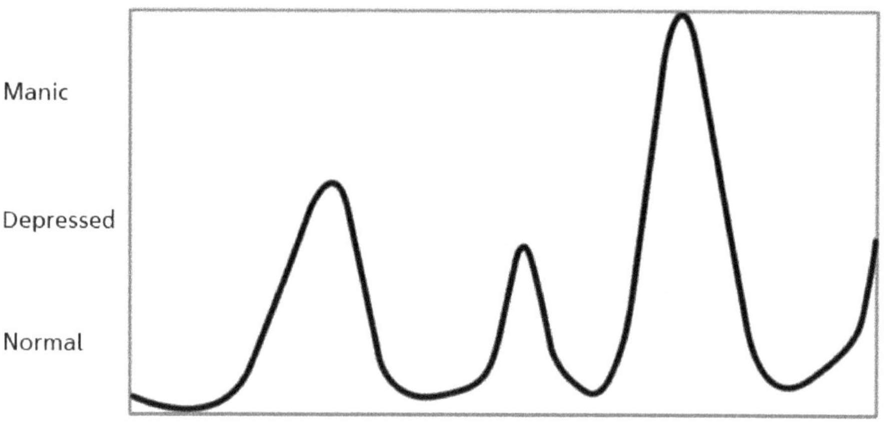

The Continuum model

This concept was posited in 1968 by a very talented young man called JH Court who would go on to have an illustrious career as an internationally regarded counsellor and psychologist. (I know him later as 'Dad.')

The difference, and it's a *huge* difference, is that the depressed state occurs immediately *before* and *after* the creative or active peak. There is no real time in the 'normal' either side of our impassioned, active creative 'high'.

So, even before you create, even before you act, before you perform your art, you will go through a period of 'down.' Robin Williams has spoken of his need to go to the toilet before going on stage for a big show, a sort of pre creative purge. (Actors studio) Many professional sporting teams will have players who are known for their pre-game rituals of throwing up, spending time in the toilet, or just pacing back and forth feeling unworthy. The same is true of actors, comedians, even teachers and preachers. Yes, some of this may be nervousness and anxiety, but a lot of it is also the pre-creation crouching down. An emotional suppression as the human machine gets ready to spring into excited, even manic, action.

Then you hit the stage. The whistle goes to start the game. The page before you is ready to take the work in your mind. The canvas is ready and so are you. Within moments any lethargy, physical suppression or tiredness is gone and, what in bipolar is called the manic phase, whisks you away. Sometimes this will be identifiable as flow, but it doesn't necessarily go that far.

And so you create.

But then the energy subsides, the game ends, the match finishes, the comedian comes off stage. See the football players after the game, the preacher after their sermon, the teacher after their lecture, the band backstage after the gig, the actors taking off the greasepaint. They are in that state again. Depressed is probably the wrong word because of the clinical baggage attached to it. Maybe 'supressed' is a better way of seeing it. If you have ever performed, played, created at a high personal level, you will know this post exertion suppression. Certainly, some of it is physical, but an enormous amount of it is emotional. You are spent. Physically and mentally. Being in the flow, in the game, in the mental discipline of creativity, is mentally taxing. Your brain gets tired, just like the athlete's body does. So you just need to stop. To rest. To power down. And slowly you begin to emerge again, back to normal.

Can you see how this continuum model is a much more realistic and logical metaphor for the creative life? Creativity is an incredibly intense mental and sometimes physical pursuit, so it's natural that, beforehand, your body will store up energy for the effort. Then afterwards, you are spent. You have done your work and your brain and body need to wind down. It natural. It's normal. It's the way we are created to operate. Kay Redfield Jamison notes that,

> The rhythms and cycles of manic-depressive illness, a singularly cyclic disease, are strikingly similar to those of the natural world, as well as to the death-and-

> regeneration and dark-and-light cycles so often captured in poetry, music and painting. (6)

To recognise this allows you to see some very important understandings.

One: You *will* be down before you get 'up'.

If you are on your way to the studio to record your new album, your body and brain will be resting up and conserving the energy it knows you will soon need. Sitting in the car on the way there, or on the way to play the grand final, you can very easily be overcome by the incredible weight of how hopelessly inadequate you feel for the job ahead. Why? Because you don't feel ready. And you are right! Your body is not ready. But that's okay, it doesn't need to be. Not in the car on the way there. Your brain and body are crouching down ready to spring to great heights. It's getting ready to work like a, well, like a maniac. A little later we'll look at 'imposter syndrome' but for now, recognise that in this stage, in this pre-creative down time, that's when it will sneak up on you and try to drag you down. Remind yourself what is really happening, and you can put your imposter syndrome back in its box.

Two: Expect to be down afterwards.

Many performers find the only way to maintain the 'up' in this situation is to medicate for it. Obviously, this is a very dangerous precedent. You *need* the down time. So use it. Tell your family and loved ones that you are in that phase, tell your fans to wait ten minutes before you meet them after the gig, and give yourself time to just be 'down.' I have seen this in churches, when the preacher is at the pulpit doing their creative best to inspire and engage. They expend enormous energy as they do. And then they are expected to stand at the door and shake hands with every single person and interact with them, up and friendly. And it's a killer. I know of a number of ministers who now, deliberately, take a break after the service and then emerge to be with their flock. The difference is they have now had time to move through their down phase.

Three: Everyone is different.

You will experience the ups and downs but you will experience them differently and you will need to find your own, personal, ways to work with them. When I first started digging into this I was amazed at how many truly successful and effective creative people time-tabled their creativity, and the process around it. Internationally renowned song writer and performer Curt Anderson once told me how he creates so prolifically. 'Frankly, I schedule it… stick in on the calendar, and go do it… and I find I'm so much more creative in those times.' Professional artists of all types would agree. Many may be surprised to find out it's what they do. I was stunned when I realised it's how I actually operated. I schedule intense work and I schedule 'down time'. When I worked as a breakfast radio presenter, I would use my pre and post show down time to ride my bike. I didn't plan it that way but riding to and from the studio used the creative down time for healthy, stress releasing exercise. I like to think this is what Albert Einstein meant when he told his son, Edouard that 'It is the same with people as it is with riding a bike. Only when moving can one comfortably maintain one's balance.' (in Irvine, 64)

Scheduling your creative time and your down time clearly utilises what we know of creativity and its ups and down. Again, Kay Redfield Jamison puts it neatly:

> The ability to reconcile such opposite states, whether they are of mood, thought, or vitality, is a critical part of any creative act. (128)

Another reason I am suspicious of the sine wave model of bipolar when applied to the creative life, is that it makes "Depressed", *beneath* normal. You go through normal and "fall into" this parlous state called depression. But no. The continuum model suggests that depression, down, suppressed mood, is *part* of the *good*, natural process. Expect it. Use it.

If you were constantly in a hyper state, you would burn out, burn up. And be a complete horror to live with. Just as always being down is bad, always being up is extremely unhealthy. The skill for the creative life is simple:

Embrace your 'down' time.

Your personal 'down' time. I have developed the ability to almost predict when I will get more than just a bit down, but will have a day of 'depression'. They are regular, consistent and quite acceptable. They are days when I know I won't get a lot of creative work done. They are days and times when I will not be drawn into pondering my failings, my emotional or financial weakness, because I know I won't be thinking clearly. I tend to clean the house or read books. I tell myself these are my 'absorbing' times because I only take things in, I 'fill the well' as we'll see later. This is also a really cool way of saying it's okay to veg out in front of the TV. Also, I tell my partner clearly where I am at, so she doesn't think it's something she has done!

I want to make it clear that being a bit depressed, sometimes, is not a problem, it's a blessing, just as being 'a bit manic' can be. And to add that expecting a low point before and after a creative explosion, or performance, is extremely wise. It *will* happen. Expect it. Plan for it. Embrace it.

Ups and Downs are *both* vital to the creative process.

But the world doesn't like that does it? Why is it so hard to embrace your down time?

Perhaps Max Weber, the German thinker, nailed it when he pointed out that the thing driving the capitalist world is what we now call 'The protestant work ethic.' We see it in common cultural touchstones such as 'A fair day's pay for a fair day's work,' and 'watch the pennies and the pounds will look after themselves' or, in Weber's own words 'Remember that *time* is money' (48) and 'Labour must... be performed as if it were an absolute end in itself, a calling.' (62)

The idea is simple and profound. Work harder and you will be more successful. It points to this cultural belief that means if you're not working, you're not worthwhile. Jerry Saltz in his book *How to Be An Artist* suggests much the same thing, saying when you,

> have tried every conceivable way to conquer work-block – that fear of working, which is a fear of failure. There's only one method that works: just work. And keep working... work is the only thing that banishes the curse of fear. (19)

He suggests that if you don't work hard you fail. But is that true?

Noting the continuum model we looked at before, we can see that we all experience the need for the down time, that period of *not* working. In fact, it is vital to our wellbeing. Even God, after spending a week creating, took a day off. A whole day, and all he did was rest. It is ironic that the thing that stops us mere humans from resting is named a 'protestant' work ethic, an ethic supposedly born from a religious movement. Humans need to work and to create in order to be engaged in life. Jerry Saltz's point is not wrong. Work *is* a key to success. But we also need to rest, to just stop creating, to embrace our 'down time.'

What must also be stated clearly is that the Protestant Work Ethic is not a protestant religious thing. Weber points this out in his book but many others have since repeated his view, such as this observation.

> Muslim Turks who live in the US believe that if they work hard they would also be successful and their work should be rewarded, and if they don't work hard enough they should be ready to accept the consequences. (Zulifkar, 502)

So let's just call it the 'Work Ethic' and not blame it on one particular race, colour, or creed. Or perhaps 'The Must Work Ethic', the cultural expectation we all take on that says if you're not working, you're not worthwhile. It's pretty easy for anyone to fall into it. And it's not a good place to fall. There are so many examples of how bad this 'Must Work Ethic' is. We need to free ourselves from the self-destructive, creativity sapping, soul destroying drive to constantly be 'on', to always be at the work.

In the next chapters we'll walk through ways in which all this can be done as you unleash your creative power and safely, effectively, and powerfully, be your creative best.

It All Boils Down to This:

Remodelling the Bipolar thing.

- Being highly creative and highly active will leave you feeling suppressed. Accept that this is a good thing.
- The suppression often occurs before you get into the creative work as well. Be prepared for it and don't worry. You can develop creative habits that will kick in when needed.
- Embrace your down time. Use it for less creative but equally valuable 'life' stuff.
- Be aware of the cultural drive to always work and recognise when you are falling into it unhealthily.

Anderson, Curt. In conversation, video. 2019

Angelou, Maya. In *Paris Review IV.* Rushdie, Salman (ed). Picador. Pp 250-271. 1990

Brown, Tim. In *Great TED talks; creativity.* May, Tom (ed) Portico. 2020.

Court, John H. Manic-depressive Psychosis: an alternative conceptual model. *British Journal of Psychiatry*. Vol 114 No. 517. Pp 1523-1530. December 1968

Crabbe, Robin Wallace. In *Studio: Australian Painters on the nature of Creativity.* Lloyd, R. Ian and McDonald, John. (Producers) R. Ian Lloyd Productions. Tower Books. 2007

Doctrow, E.L. *Writers at Work – Sixth Series*. Plimpton, George (ed) Penguin. 1985

Einstein, Albert. *Quote investigator.* https://quoteinvestigator.com/2015/06/28/bicycle/ Retrieved 08 09 2022

Finn, Tim. In *Songwriters speak. Conversations about creating music.* Krueger, Debbie. (ed) Limelight Press. 2005

Irvine, Ben. *Einstein and the Art of Mindful Cycling.* Leaping Hare Press. 2018

Jamison, Kay Redfield. *Touched With Fire. Manic Depressive illness and the artistic temperament.* Free press. 1993

Pritchett, V.*S. Midnight Oil,* Vintage. *1971*

Saltz, Jerry. *How to be an artist.* Hachette. 2020

Thuys, Erik. Fragile and Fruitful Minds: Creativity and Psychopathology. in *New Frontiers in Creativity*. Kreitler, Shulamith (ed) Nova science. 2020.

Weber, Max. *The protestant ethic and the spirit of capitalism.* Talcott Parsons, (Trans) 2nd ed. George Allen and Unwin. 1976

Williams, Robin. *Inside the actors Studio.* Dir: Jeff Wurtz. EP: James Lipton. Gryphon Entertainment. 2008

Woodley, Bruce. In *Songwriters speak. Conversations about creating music.* Krueger, Debbie (ed) Limelight Press. 2005

Zulifkar, Yavuv Fahir. Do Muslims believe more in protestant work ethic than Christians? Comparison of people with different religious background living in the US. *Journal of Business Ethics.* Vol 105. Pp 489-502. 2012.

A word about...
Creating Armageddon. The Moral Question.

Creativity has enormous power. Apparently. Especially when that creativity is unleashed unwisely. Sir Mark Oliphant, who lived just around the corner from where I grew up, had a huge impact on science, like radar, the development of nuclear energy and much more. Most prominent is his involvement in The Manhattan Project. The creation of the first functional nuclear weapon. If you saw the film *Oppenheimer*, you'll not see much of Sir Mark. Perhaps because, after he played a pivotal role in the development of the most destructive weapon ever, he backed away and roundly condemned the work they had done. He refused to join the British program and was constantly pushing for the peaceful use of the amazing technology that had come from his astounding scientific creativity. He said of himself, 'During the war I worked practically the whole time on defence research. I worked then on nuclear weapons so I, too, am a war criminal.' (Cockburn) And herein lies a question this book *doesn't* answer. How do you consider the moral impact of your creative work? I don't go into it here because it's a four-volume discussion on its own, but every creator probably needs to consider what their work will bring to the world. Good and bad. Imagine if no one had created pornography? Imagine if the person involved had decided not to write 'Baby Shark'? Imagine if Sir Mark had stepped away from the British MAUD committee that eventually helped weaponise nuclear energy? Imagine if he hadn't joined the Manhattan Project?

For a start, he wouldn't have become 'Sir Mark' and someone else might well have done the work anyway, but he would not be responsible... and so the whole moral merry-go-round turns. This is not an attempt to give you the answer, or the solution, but rather to raise the question, as you become more and more impacting in your creative life. What impact are you trying to achieve? And what impact is occurring coincidentally? Do you think the inventors of the computer phenomenon *Minecraft* said 'we want to create a generation of screen potatoes?' It is just this sort of self-questioning that led Sir Mark to say, 'I believe the trouble with the modern applications of science is that they can yield guns as well as butter.'

Cockburn, Stewart and Ellyard, David. *Oliphant. The life and Times of Sir Mark Oliphant.* Axiom. 1981

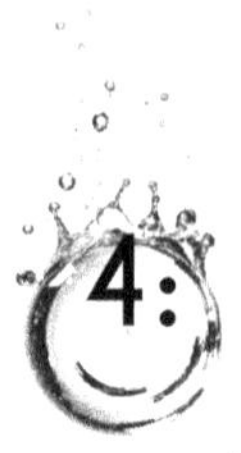

Gotta love the weird.

Disequilibrium and being 'wrong'.

> You have to be dissatisfied with something in order to want to improve it, to seek a better way. That's why the creative mind is endlessly restless: it's always trying to solve a problem or do something in a better way. (73)
>
> ROGER MAVITY

The piles of books, podcasts, or talks on creativity, all look at various aspects of how to create and how to push aside the things that stop you creating. Those are all really useful things and if you want those things, skip forward a few pages and we'll get into them. However, before you get there it's important to remember that, as we've mentioned, everyone is different. So what works for the author or podcaster of the day, may be wrong for you. That's why we've been spending a little time pottering about behind the creative scenes. Now let's move forward to look at some of the things that really matter to your creativity. First, we need to address the big question you didn't even realise was there.

Why?

The process of creativity, the ways of freeing creativity up and the product of creativity are all kind of secondary. Sure, they feel vital and we're digging into all of that, but there is one thing that matters more.

If you're walking down the street, you just walk. You don't really think about breathing right? You know why you breathe but you don't concentrate on it. But if you fall off a boat and you're flailing about in the water you will try to swim, or at least float. This time you know exactly why you are doing what you are doing. Breathing has become very top of mind. It's so you don't drown! When it comes to creating, why do you do it? If you can't put a handle on that you'll be flailing about trying to express… something. For the inventor with a vision or the advertising writer, even the speech making politician, the 'why' may seem obvious. They have a message that they are trying to express. But wait. *Why* are they trying to express it? Because it's their job? Their passion? Okay, sure… but *why* is communicating like this your passion?

And why is the poet staring into space with a pencil in her mouth? Why is the painter furiously arguing with the colours on their palette? Why is the guitarist anxious to get this lyric, this tone just right?

One word keeps popping up in this area. The art, the heart, the brain that makes change is one that has a need to make change. It is a heart and soul in a state of:

Disequilibrium.

Something is wrong, or at least out of whack. Often this will express itself as a general social malaise or a dissatisfaction with 'the way things are'. This disequilibrium not only gives rise to creativity, but it can also be seen as the thing that gives rise to whole new artistic movements, new methods of doing things, from surgery to landscaping, it turns painters into impressionists, musicians into punks. It is a force within us driving us to do. Artist and critic Jerry Saltz speaks of this, telling artists that,

> Imagination is your creed, sentimentality and lack of feeling are your foes. All art comes from love-love of doing something… Even if we're in agony while we're working, it's still some kind of love that drives us on against the current. (9)

For those who find themselves driven to write, you'll recognise the sentiment expressed by Helen Garner. 'I write to unburden myself, to amuse myself, to arrange in order the things that bulge in my head, to make myself notice things.' (2)

It is that bulge in the head, the need to order things, that love, that makes us create even when it hurts, when we are down, disheartened, oppressed by the world, whatever, we just gotta do it. To put it a different way:

Creativity isn't so much what you do… it's as much who you *are*.

This is especially important to the artist creator. Whereas a scientist may be seeking a creative way to explain, say, the nature of DNA, an artist may feel within themselves a disgust of injustice, or a discomfort with waking up late, or they look at stuff and say 'what if' and 'I wonder.' Disequilibrium doesn't have to be a solid identifiable 'thing'. It's more likely a whole lot of little things that just seem… kind of like I want to change them or play with them. We'll talk later about why play is so important to being a human but perhaps right here we begin to see it. Think of Play dough, right? Is there anything 'wrong' with it? No, but we are pretty much driven to pick it up and shape it into something else. Why? Because that's what we do. We change things, we create new things. It's a human drive. Unlike the artist, the scientist, the business thinker, even the marketing guru, are all operating in a realm where the target outcome is specific and bounded. In Chapter one we labelled this PC. Problem-solving creativity, as opposed to UC. Untethered creativity. The artist, the creator with the free-reign imagination, is not constrained by a commercial outcome, a product out-put or a technical solution. G.J. Feist makes the observation that,

> in the expressive arts, personal meaning, subjectivity, and emotion play a motivational role in ways not common in the more formal creative professions. (3)

Even more than this, the role of the artist as creator is much more personal and self-engaged. Seeking to develop a medical treatment, a solution to a sickness, is creativity within a team and field and a set of rules and regulations. Those rules will not just be ethics and acceptable behaviours, but the bounds of science and nature. The artist has almost none of this. They are self-regulated. In his book about *The Plenitude* Rich Gold points out that,

> It is traditional for artists to see themselves as agents of change attempting to bring down, or at least alter, or at least awaken, or at least offend, the ruling structures. (13)

You don't really want to offend and bring down ruling structures if you are developing a surgical intervention for cancer. But if you're creating a fantasy-world computer game, it's pretty much the job description.

This suggests that central to the creative process of the artist is a deep, abiding and driving force. A disequilibrium. When collecting the thoughts of Australian Painters, Ian McDonald, in his introduction to '*Studio*' states that 'Painting is a way of making sense of one's environment, but it is also, in its secret heart, an attempt to control and alter that environment.' (11)

The creative impetus for the scientist, the advertising writer, the creator aiming for an outcome, is quite well explored and logical. But for the artists making something because they have to, for which there is no guarantee of an outcome, the drive is something else, something much more personal. George Orwell felt that;

> Writing a book is a horrible, exhausting struggle, like a long bout of some painful illness. One would never undertake such a thing if one were not driven on by some demon whom one can neither resist nor understand. (36)

So why do we do it? Because, as every writer, painter, photographer, musician, songwriter, artist, in fact anyone who creates knows, we *have* to. It's who we are. And, as we found in the opening chapters, *everyone* is that someone. We *all* have this 'painful illness', this need to create, to be creative. When Tom McLeish looked at *Creativity, imagination and being in the image of God*, he noted that 'all creativity begins with a desire to reach a dimly perceived goal, whether that be a sonnet on a visage or the science of vision.' (5) This creative desire includes people who garden, who play sport, who make cakes, teach students, preach sermons... in fact pretty much all human activity requires a creative component. Are you wearing makeup? Clothes? Hair? All those things are choices derived from your creative imagination. The question is; do we engage effectively and powerfully with our creative self, or do we try to ignore it? And if so, why?

All of this points to one tremendously scary thing about creativity. The thing that makes many people turn away from it and shut it in a box. Creativity comes from being uncertain, uncomfortable, even. To use a loaded term; being unbalanced. Many people will back off and try to ignore this state of disequilibrium within them because it's uncomfortable. But if you wish for the creative life, don't back away. Being uncomfortable is not a bad thing. Without the discomfort and disequilibrium, you can't reach the heights your life is designed for.

As I point out to students, nothing good ever came from being comfortable. Except, perhaps, hardened arteries and a sofa with bum-dents in it. Comfort kills creativity. We'll look more at the vital need to rest, unwind and relax, later, but for now, note that if you want to be more creative, stop closing your eyes to the things you don't like.

There is a 'why' inside us all, a disequilibrium that drives us to create. For many people the disequilibrium may not be an existential world sized crisis. It may just be a deadline.

American satirist Garrison Keilor allegedly has said he loves deadlines, especially the delightful whooshing noise they make as they sail past. But many students will be familiar with the boost of effectiveness that comes the night before an assignment is due. Many people, myself included, are well aware of the added pressure of a looming deadline and the usefulness of that pressure. There are few creators who do not recognise the value of a deadline for putting some urgency into their creativity. To quote the song; 'Death inspires me like a dog inspires the rabbit.' (21 Pilots) A deadline inspires me the same way.

Some people find this more than others. And it will probably differ at different times for each individual. The roar of the approaching deadline can often be a deafening distraction, or it can be the driving force. For advertising creative guru David Abbot, the approaching deadline may have been just what he needed. Roger Mavity tells this story:

> David's surface demeanour was one of astonishing calm and control. But when he needed to produce an advertising campaign, he became a master of procrastination. On one occasion, we had three weeks to produce ideas for a new campaign. After three weeks minus one day, David had nothing to show. The presentation was booked for 9 a.m. the following day. I asked David how it was going. 'Nothing yet,' he said.

> 'You'll just have to be a bit patient. I've got other stuff today, but I'll do it at home tonight.' The next morning, I came in half an hour before the meeting and waited anxiously. With ten minutes to go, I heard David's car come into the car park. He stepped into the office with a sheaf of drawings under his arm. He spread them out in front of me, and they were brilliant. 'My God,' I said, 'you had a productive evening last night.' 'Not really,' he replied. 'I couldn't get any decent ideas last night, so I went to bed, got up at five this morning, and then the ideas flowed.' (42-43)

Cool story and all that, but two things must be noted about this way of creating.

One: It relies on enormous self-confidence, that the ideas will come as needed. And Two: It's going to crush the people around you, who rely on you but aren't as comfortable as you. But more on all of that later. For now, this all goes to highlight the fact that if there is a devil on our tail we run faster and create more efficiently. It points to the value of disequilibrium as a driving force for creativity.

Sometimes.

Sometimes it works. But sometimes it actually works against you. Whilst disequilibrium may well give you the desire to rail against something, to have something to say, it is possible that this drive will also run you into the ground. Likewise, if you are constantly operating on the edge of your deadlines, is this a healthy way to carry out your life? And what about those around you, who are relying on you to provide the product? Or who need you to be mummy or daddy, or partner? Can *they* survive your constant deadline dancing?

In fact, as a way of creating, pushing deadlines can be a terribly draining process and one that removes from creativity one of its greatest values.

Being creative is a gift, a joy, a wonderful thing that is unique to you, for you to enjoy and thrive with. If you are constantly allowing your creativity to push you to the edge of stress and failure, are you really getting the most from it? Or, as Jeff Crabtree says:

> … Artistry and creativity exist to serve higher ends than our own personal drives. Even though creatives of all disciplines will invest huge amounts of time, money and energy to achieve their personal goals, deep down every one of them knows they are the recipient of a gift. Their talent – the raw potential to develop skill in a creative discipline – was a gift. (180)

So, you may feel weird as a creator because the reason you create is born of the knowledge that the world in which you live is in need of a good kicking. Or at least a good questioning. On that point, let me return to the first principle. *Everyone* is creative and all of us know things need to be questioned and even kicked a bit. Some of us are less inclined to do that kicking and this may point to why some people feel less creative. Roger Mavity suggests, 'Creativity is only achieved by those in a high state of dissatisfaction.' (76)

Maybe being angry helps you create? Maybe, but not likely. And the research here is pretty clear. Also, being comfortable, relaxed and at ease, probably won't help. Let me unpack that for you because it's central.

So-called activating positive moods, such as elation, were found to be associated with higher levels of creativity, whereas deactivating positive moods, such as serenity, were not. Being pumped and excited unleashes your creativity, just being reflective and quiet doesn't of itself, help creativity. Patrick Bateson wrote about how moods tangle with your creativity. His findings;

> ran counter to the common belief that creative ideas emerge when people are relaxing. Furthermore, Baas et al. (2008) found suggestive evidence that some mood states, such as feeling happy, may generate original ideas through enhanced fluency, whereas others, such as anger, may exert their effects through enhanced persistence with the task. This difference makes sense in terms of the distinction we have drawn between

> generating new ideas (creativity) and turning those ideas into practical solutions that are adopted by others (innovation). (94)

So, in different people, different moods have different impacts on their creative output, but generally, freedom to create with a sense of pressure, i.e. a deadline or an internal drive for excellence, will likely create the most fluent, original and impacting creative output. Whereas being driven by anger or external factors such as the need to prove yourself, or just to be done with it, will increase the amount of work but decrease its originality, its novelty. Interestingly, the state of being relaxed, or comfortable in the creative act, did nothing to enhance the process. This supported evidence that a measure of threat or emotional discomfort is vital to driving the internal engine of highly effective creativity. Andrew Jaroz goes on about this with research that suggests;

> Increased attentional control implies that one is better able to screen out peripheral information, which, while useful during analytical problem solving, would be disadvantageous in a situation where the assimilation of information outside of the perceived problem space may be useful… it is reasonable to suggest that in the case of creative problem solving, less attentional control may in fact be beneficial to solution (488)

In other words, the person who is landing your plane better be focused entirely on the act and the processes of landing that plane. If they are admiring the clouds or daydreaming of a strawberry sundae, you can all end up dead. We prefer they use the intense focus of executive function.

But if you are composing a sonnet, imagining the next scene in your screen play or designing a wedding cake, the truly creative outcome requires you to have *everything* on the emotional table. If you are designing new packaging for a strawberry sundae, why NOT daydream about landing a plane? Who knows what inspirations it may elicit? Which makes perfect sense. Andrew Jarosz spent some time researching the effects of alcohol on problem solving. Properly, not just for fun. He noted that, 'Previous research has suggested that a deficit in executive functioning can provide benefits in creative tasks.' (490) Daydreaming, wandering thoughts, the flight of ideas, are brilliant for creative unleashing. Not so good for your pilot.

Clearly, there are times and mental places, where creative process takes us to places where the rest of the world, the day to day, may be unhelpful. When writing about stealing creative fire, Stephen Bayley points out his belief that 'The workmanlike craft of execution may be just as important to the act of genius as the whack-job creative concept.' (6) For some of us, part of the disequilibrium and unbalance we feel may be that core need to be chasing crazy dreams and the need to make them into valuable works. Therefore, 'perhaps one of the greatest enemies of the creative mind is indifference, because the deep resources of emotion and passion are where the stuff that drives the creative mind comes from.' (Crabtree, 91)

To answer the question from chapter one, what is the opposite of being creative? Perhaps it is 'being comfortable.'

A word about...
Plotters and Pantsers and Option paralysis.

There is an ongoing discussion amongst writers about the validity and quality of work created by 'Pantsers,' those who just go with their feelings, by the seat of their pants, versus the 'Plotters,' those who map, plan and structure before they begin. Now, the fact is *both* are essential to a final work. It's like nature versus nurture. It is nature *and* nurture. But the discussion underlines one of the major factors in what is called writers block, painters block, singers block, whatever it is for you. The thing that stops us starting. Let me show you how it works.

I wake up every morning and make tea. Okay, easy. Until I married a woman who *really* loves tea. In many styles, types and varieties. Now I wake and ask her 'What tea would you like this morning?' And I wait ten minutes for her to decide. This means two things. One; I get an extra ten minutes lazing in bed and Two; too many choices has caused option paralysis. It is why writing prompts are so useful for getting started, why notebooks come in handy and why an idea can strike and carry you away. Option paralysis occurs when you have so many options you can't choose just one. Like if I say 'Pick a word', you can't because there are so many options, no boundaries, no direction. Pick a number. Same thing, unless I say pick a number between one and ten. It's what happens when many of us see a restaurant menu. We choose. Then change our minds, then end up ordering the same thing every time. Option paralysis. For your thriving creative life, it is really good to know what is happening but, more importantly, how to beat it down. Simply put, option paralysis often comes down to 'best'. The question posed by the restaurant menu is 'what will be the best'? The problem is, you don't *know* because you haven't had it yet, and also you are trying to weigh up things you haven't even seen. For me option paralysis can kill my creative flow when I need a name. I start a story and the protagonist walks into a bar, for example, and says "Hi my name is..." I know the name is vital. Central even to their persona. But I haven't written them yet, so every option is on the table, I can give them any name I want. And I can get stuck because I don't want them to have just any name. I want them to have the *best* name. But I don't know what that will be yet. So I'm stuck. The solution is simple. Ignore it. Most of my characters spend a lot of time as 'Blob'. So Blob orders a drink at the bar. Because if I try to overcome the option paralysis now, I'll never get any further. The name is not ready yet, so I put Blob in the picture knowing, and trusting, that as the story unfolds, so will his actual name. Paralysis avoided. Because I have learned to trust the edit and to trust the ambiguity. The other problem is 'best' is what you make it. When my wife tries to decide which tea she wants, it takes ages because she is trying to decide which tea will be 'best' this morning. The reality is it doesn't matter! She has already selected all the teas we have because she paid money for them. They have all been deemed good enough, so she can't really go wrong. It's the same with every option I face in my creative life. I have skill, domain experience and the knowledge to keep the process going so every choice I make is going to be good. And if it's not, I edit it out later. Goodbye Blob. To put it more poetically, the airplane in my heads needs a destination before it can take off, but I might not land it there. The best choice in any creative process is the one you make, the one that keeps you processing forward. Option paralysis kills the creative process when you forget you are in the middle of something, not the end, and when you believe that everything you do has to be your best. Always. Not true. Creativity is a process, and you can always change things later. Unless you let it paralyse you.

We create because we feel something is wrong, or driving us, or we need to just do something and say something. This disequilibrium powers us. But here we find another interesting correlation. Even as we try to create from a place of 'wrong', unbalanced, unsettled, whatever you call it, what we create is wrong too. Let me explain, because it's another of those things that flies in the face of assumed knowledge.

> Research on creativity shows that truly successful innovative thinking, the kind that creates profitable commercial successes, is not done by chaotic brainstorming. Rather, practical creativity is highly disciplined, built on hard work, with clear milestones and goals, and a systematic process. (Maital, 43)

To thrive as a highly creative person, (AKA: a Human) you need to be able to hold both of these states. Chaos and discipline. The most obvious example for many is the working novelist or the songwriter. The free roaming, note taking, flash of inspiration that just flies off the fingers in that state of flow we talked about earlier, creates a lot of tremendously valuable chaotic raw material. But it's raw. Every published author I have ever met agrees with the notion that writing takes about 20% of the time and effort. The other 80% is re-writing, editing, revising. Musicians will concur. The flighty weird bit, the 20%, is followed by the executive function of the editing and arranging, the 80%. In our creative writing and communications courses the common refrain is that anyone can write. Few people can be authors. Because;

Writers just write. Authors Edit.

The process, remember it's a process, is untethered creativity *plus* the deliberate executive function of problem solving creativity, together.

And that brings us to the wrong. We'll look at this more shortly, but, as you can see, the process of creativity and creating a 'thing' means that, for a very long time, the 'thing' is wrong. It's not finished yet. It's in process. This is the core of things like imposter syndrome and is one of the more debilitating realities of creating high quality work. When you're in it, it feels like this work is not good enough. And you're absolutely right! Of course it's not good enough. It's not finished yet. The world is full of stories of inventors trying dozens of permutations before finally making the 'thing', of so many successful authors leaving the 'thing' aside because they didn't believe in it, frustrated roars at a song that just won't be good enough… before it becomes a classic. The novelist Anne Lamott would tell you that 'Every writer you know writes terrible first drafts, but they keep their butt in the chair.' (157) My colleague and author of over 60 novels, Anne Clark, refers to these 'terrible first drafts', as vomit drafts. Just spewed out, untidy and messy. This is where you need to cling to the fact: Creativity is a process. What you're creating is not a 'thing'. Until it is.

So are you good with weirdness? Can you live with 'wrong'? We've already noted that we create because we feel or sense some disequilibrium. Also, the very process of creating a thing, making art, or a product, or bringing an idea to fruition, means that you have to live in the wrongness of it. As you create the work, it's in process, being made, so it's not yet complete. And that feels weird. In fact, even when it's finished, it's not finished.

Chapter seven looks at failing and why it's an important thing, and I'll introduce you to the ugly baby theory, but for now let's get comfortable with the weirdness of being wrong. It can be an uncomfortable place to be. But as a creator it's a place you're going to live. If your art, your work, makes you feel uncomfortable, good. It may just be the best thing ever. You see, the disequilibrium that drives you is not likely to be resolved and this means you are going to be spending a lot of time in that land of discomfort, that place of wrongness. Here's the good news. Without that place of discomfort, you're unlikely to create brilliance. Comfort breeds mediocrity. Discomfort breeds growth and excellence. How do I know? Because brilliant creators have said so, like Toni Morrison, who says 'I write the way women have babies. You don't know it's going to be like that. If you did, there's no way you would go through with it.' (37)

In light of what we found in the earlier chapters, this wrongness, weirdness and disequilibrium makes perfect sense.

> Creative people live with opposites. At the core of this tension is this opposition of moods of mania and depression… From this place comes a voice that can touch the hearts and souls of millions. (Crabtree, 69)

Feeling better about being weird now? The Crabtree's don't talk about finding a balance, and I think that's vitally important. The idea of finding a balance means constantly self-checking and regulating and altering your behaviour to meet some abstract and possibly erroneous belief about what is 'right'. Your creative life is not about balance, it's about coming to terms with a life that may, to others seem out of balance. In *Living with a Creative Mind* Jeff and Julia Crabtree make the point that what you are doing is not being unbalanced but rather living with a life of tides. They come and go, in and out. This is not a picture of wild, uncomfortable mood swings, even though at times that's how it may look and feel, but rather you are living with a regular tidal flow, high tide to low tide then back again, across the domains of your personality.

So let me wrap this bit up. Here's the weirdness that makes creativity seem so odd. It's a direct contradiction. You need to decide for yourself when you sit on which side of this contradiction.

The 'weird' side: Is well expressed by most highly effective creators but summed up nicely by Li Huang who did a bunch or research looking at how just making yourself feel weird physically can unleash creativity. He found that,

> it is OK to feel awkward or uncomfortable—that in fact, this is the point... In short, activities that disrupt your habituated, authentic body language can trigger an unconventional mindset and help encourage creative insights and resilience. (Huang)

But sometimes you need to be in the place where that weirdness becomes a successful, shareable product. Where the strange thinking about electricity becomes the lightbulb, where the alien becomes a novel, or the talking cat becomes a cartoon strip. Cristina Domenech, in a TED talk encouraging us to *Harness dark feelings to be more creative*, confirms the idea that embracing your weird, being okay with the uncomfortable, can be incredibly powerful for your creativity. She states that, '…we all have our dark emotions and bad memories. Dig deep, draw on them and you might just make something transformational as a result.' (May, 82)

Living with the reality of your constantly shifting self is a lifestyle choice that will bear great creative fruit. It unleashes the free form flow of ideas but also means you're not a slave to the uncertainty, the unbalanced and the disequilibrium. Do you really want balance? Or does the truly powerful come from the complexity and contradiction?

It All Boils Down To This:

Gotta love the weirdness

- Creativity isn't just what you do, it's as much what you are.
- Know why you create. What drives you?
- Living your creativity can be unsettling and that can cause you to back off.
- Nothing good ever came from being comfortable.
- Deadlines don't have to be bad.
- When we create, it's 'bad' because it's not finished yet, and that's okay.
- Writers write, authors edit.

21 Pilots. *Heavy Dirty soul.* Tyler Joseph. Warner Chappell Music. 2016

Bateson, Patrick and Martin, Paul. *Play, Playfulness, creativity and innovation.* Cambridge. 2013

Bayley, Stephen and Mavity, Roger. *How to steal fire.* Bantam. 2019

Crabtree, Jeff. Crabtree, Julia. *Living with a creative mind.* Zebra Collective. 2011

Domench, Cristina. In *Great TED talks; creativity.* May, Tom (ed) Portico. 2020.

Feist, G. J., Dostal, D., & Kwan, V. Psychopathology in World-Class Artistic and Scientific Creativity. *Psychology of Aesthetics, Creativity, and the Arts*. Advance online publication. http://dx.doi.org/10.1037/aca0000440. 2021

Garner, Helen. *Yellow Notebook: Diaries volume one 1978-1987.* Text publishing. 2019

Gold, Rich. *The Plenitude: Creativity, Innovation, and Making Stuff.* MIT Press. 2007

Huang, Li. Being your authentic self is actually not ideal for creativity. *Qz.com*, https://qz.com/work/2035693/being-your-authentic-self-is-not-ideal-for-creativity/ 20 March 2022

Jarosz, Andrew F, Colflesh, and Wiley, Jennifer. Uncorking the muse: Alcohol intoxication facilitates creative problem solving. *Consciousness and Cognition*. Vol 21. Pp 487–493. 2012

Lamott, Anne. In *Great TED talks; creativity.* May, Tom (ed) Portico. 2020.

Maital, Shlomo and Ruttenberg, Ari. *Cracking the creativity code.* Sage publications. 2014

Mavity, Roger and Bayley, Stephen. *How to steal fire.* Bantam. 2019

McDonald, John. Introduction. *Studio: Australian painters on the nature of creativity.* R. Ian Lloyd Productions. Tower Books. 2007

McLeish, Tom. Creativity, imagination and being in the image of God: a Précis of The Poetry and Music of Science. *Interdisciplinary Science Reviews.* 45:1, 1-7, DOI: 10.1080/03080188.2020.1730099. 2020

Orwell, George. *The Quotable Book Lover*. Ben Jacobs and Helena Hjalmarsson (eds) Skyhorse publishing. 1999

Saltz, Jerry. *How to be an artist.* Hachette. 2020

Who's got the Cultural Curse?

> In short to come up with inventive and creative ideas, you need to free your mind from the judgement of others...
>
> TIM BROWN. IDEO

Possibly one of the greatest challenges to thriving as a highly effective creative person, is recognising what is stopping you. It makes sense that if you have been created to be creative, if you are driven by some disequilibrium to create, and if you are beginning to understand the flows and fluxes in your own process, with all that understood, surely you should just... do it? Right?

But often we don't. And even when we have created, or when we are in the middle of our creative practice, there are things holding us back and tripping us up. It often feels as if the single most powerful device in our creative life is the handbrake.

Let's have a look at what that hand brake might be and see if we can't release it. To become a highly effective creative powerhouse, we've already started looking at what you need to know about what's making you the creative way you are. But here's another big factor. Culture. That invisible, impossible to avoid, undefined, all encompassing, collection of family, friends, neighbours, desires, expectations and 'natural' beliefs that have allowed you get to this stage.

What is the world around you doing to your creativity?

This book has been largely written on Kaurna land, although this particular piece is being constructed in the Adelaide Hills, on Permangk land. This is an understanding that the place I sit and write is a place that means something vastly different to another culture, the indigenous people that have been on this land for thousands of years before white people decided our culture was better. Long story short, a lot of damage was done, people died and the land, and all of us who live on it, suffer because we have failed to understand the land and the culture that has gone before. As I write this, there is talk around me of impending bushfires, destructive floods and crops failing because the crops are not from here. These are the result of centuries of cultural blindness. It's an understanding that is only very new to me. It is also heavily political and heavily contested. Culture is like that. 'Us' versus 'Them' and all that. Into each little nook and cranny of culture, people are growing and shaping. And creating. Each one of us is doing so grounded in our own beliefs and 'truths'. These truths can be incredibly hard to see but also incredibly important and, therefore, tightly held. Witness the folk at the French satirical magazine *Charlie Hebdo,* whose free French libertarian culture led them to creatively mock Muhammed, The profit of the Islamic faith. In 2015 their free form fun met the culture of radical fundamentalist Islam. The result was the death of 12 people as the fundamentalists sought to defend their culture from another culture that was expressing itself. Who was right? It depends who you ask, and which culture their feet have been rooted in. Most cultural clashes are less extreme than this, but it really draws attention to the problem for a creative person. Culture is incredibly powerful. The previous bit of this book looked at how creativity is, at its most basic, a force within us driven by a disequilibrium, a need to correct the unbalance. Both the satirists at *Charlie Hebdo* and the gunmen who sought to silence them, were expressing their disequilibrium in the best way they could see, using their most effective weapon. The reason this disequilibrium can be so hard to identify is because it is embedded in our very beings. Our entire lives have been shaped by beliefs and truths that we don't even notice. When we feel the urge to push back, I wonder, how many creative pursuits meet their first obstacle at the kitchen table? 'No, you can't be a comedian, rock star, painter etc. you need a proper job…' But conversely, how much of the disequilibrium that makes us push back, is based on the fact that you want to become a comedian, rock star, painter etc. simply to challenge the cloying, unfair and seemingly enormous discomfort that comes from being held by the truths and beliefs of your family upbringing? Youths rebel, perhaps, because they are moving beyond the culture of home.

Todd Lubart highlights a further consideration, pointing out that;

> the level of creativity permitted on a topic is often inversely related to the topic's role in the maintenance of deep cultural patterns. That is, for topics related to religion or considered as sacred in some way, there seems to be much more reluctance to change, than for topics that are taken less seriously in the culture and for which less obedience is expected. (40)

The bits of culture that are the most 'important' to a specific culture are the ones most fiercely defended, and the ones where it is hardest to be creative. Now, let me say what I'm *not* saying. I'm not saying it *should* be this way, or that this is a good way to live. It just is.

Salman Rushdie received death threats and a fatwa for his book *The Satanic Verses.* And a huge amount of free publicity. I remember seeing the singer Cat Stevens, after converting to Islam, saying he would personally be willing to carry out the fatwa, and kill Salman Rushdie. Clearly, I misunderstood the meaning of his song '*Morning has Broken.'* In 2022, Rushdie was speaking at a literary event in Chautauqua, New York, when he was attacked on stage and stabbed multiple times.

So what does this have to do with creativity?

It's a cultural clash that makes me reconsider how I create, what I create, where can my creativity go, where can't it go? Have I accidentally upset some Islamic truth? Have I offended some indigenous cultural element that I am unaware of? And therefore, should I even go there? There is a whole lot to add about cancel culture and the culture of offense we have made for ourselves, but let's leave that because it's just the latest iteration of the cultural curse in creative practice. I mentioned earlier my ignorance of indigenous culture. If I want to write a story with an indigenous element to it, I am now very leery of it, in case I end up being run through with the pointy end of someone else's personal beliefs about what I can and cannot say. Simply put, culture kills creativity because most cultural practices and cornerstones are maintained through fear. In hiding from death threats, Salman Rushdie wrote, in the third person of course, about how his clash with culture affected him.

> "I am gagged and imprisoned," he wrote in his journal. "I can't even speak. I want to kick a football in a park with my son. Ordinary, banal life: my impossible dream." Friends who saw him in those days were shocked by his physical deterioration, his weight gain, the way he had let

> his beard grow out into an ugly bulbous mass, his sunken stance. He looked like a beaten man.

Culture is an incredibly potent element of our lives, one we rarely attend to or even notice. And culture is often installed and maintained by fear. It is, therefore, not culture itself that handbrakes our creativity. It is fear. Fear kills creativity. And fear of transgressing our deepest most ingrained and valued cultural foundations has got to be a huge factor, right?

If I fear being stabbed or gunned down, I will curtail my creativity around that.

If I fear the frowns and disdain of my Christian pastor because I like to paint nudes, I will curtail my creativity.

If I fear my wife thinking I'm weird for constantly writing about murdering people, I will curtail my thriller writing.

If my record company demands hits, I will do what they say, curtailing my excursions into Tibetan nose singing, for fear of losing their support. And money.

Fear drives a lot of our creative decisions, without us even realising it. It is vital for you, as a creator, to know what is acting on your process from the cultural realm.

The problem is that, for most of us, the cultural imperative that is blocking us is not as obvious as a religious opposition or a racial divide. Whilst these 'big ticket' cultural items will always be there for all people, in all places, we will also have 'smaller' more intimate cultural and experiential effectors. Things like your favourite music, or foods, the 'right' way to dress or speak, how to have sex, how to drive, how 'silly' you can be, how to treat animals, or toys, how to treat nature... and on and on it goes. Every understanding in our lives has come from somewhere. Some of those 'somewheres' are going to drive us to great creative heights. But, equally, some of those 'somewheres' may fill us with fear.

Obviously, as the creator of a product, you need to be aware of the people that you want to buy your product. You need to be attractive to the cultural expectations of those who you want to appeal to. You need to be aware of expectations and even to meet some of them, to be a successful creator. Getting the culture right, without succumbing to its curtailing elements is going to be a full-time job. The thing is this might seem like a no-brainer. These cultural influences are called cultural norms for a reason. As Mark Runco notes;

> Culture represents a set of long-term constraints on creative thought. To fit into a culture, the individual conforms to the values of that culture, and conformity precludes the originality that is necessary for creativity. Cultures of course vary in terms of the degree of constraint (or latitude). (15)

It's kind of obvious. And that is exactly the problem. It's so obvious we forget to look for the curtailing influences of the culture we are swimming in and so go about our work with one hand tied behind our norms.

So how can you uncover your own cultural norms, the things that you take for granted? In her book about doing improv theatre, Kat Koppett touches on one aspect:

> Given the ancient, organic, and pervasive nature of storytelling in our lives, much of the training in storytelling comes down to making the unconscious processes that we already employ conscious. (67)

For those of you who love patchouli oil and adult colouring exercises, 'making the unconscious processes … conscious' is a thing that has become lauded as mindfulness. For the rest of us, it's a case of being aware, listening to yourself, knowing thyself. Kat Koppett goes on to add that 'To tell a story, we make choices about what connections to highlight, which paths to follow, and what details to focus on.' (67) It is in the making of these creative decisions that we will feel the weight of our cultural baggage. Not just in the things we do but maybe even more so in what we shy away from. If you don't feel the weight of these things, you may be playing it safe. And predictable. And for the creative life to have an impact, to address the driving equilibrium, you will *need* to feel that weight and *not* avoid it. In the world of improv theatre, Kat Koppett makes the point that, 'taboo and dangerous subject matter is the stuff of great theatre.' (13) It is also the matter of great music, great writing, great art, great… anything. In her book, she presents a list of things that were shouting at her as she wrote, a list of the negatives that were holding her back:

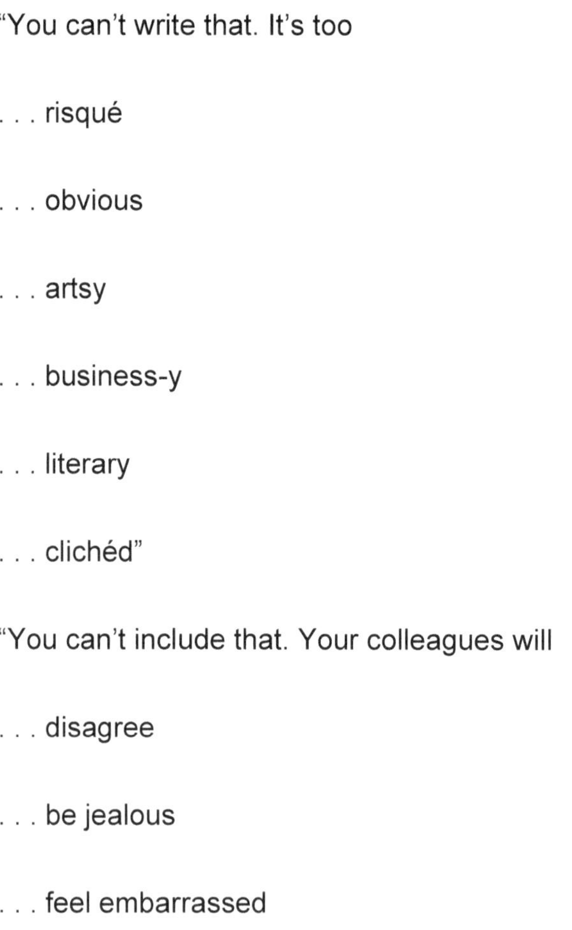

"You can't write that. It's too

. . . risqué

. . . obvious

. . . artsy

. . . business-y

. . . literary

. . . clichéd"

"You can't include that. Your colleagues will

. . . disagree

. . . be jealous

. . . feel embarrassed

. . . think you're stuck up"

Your mother will

. . . criticize your grammar

. . . misunderstand

. . . think it's bunk

(Koppett, 31)

Can you feel her problem? Do any of these things ring a bell for you? These are all cultural considerations. And every single one of them is based on a judgement derived from an external observer. Each potential 'problem' with her writing is based on the understanding of how someone else, some other peoples, or cultural responders, will view her work, even as she was creating it. Making a list like this doesn't stop those nagging fears, but it does show them up for what they really are. External. They are beyond your head and beyond your control. They do not have to be a core part of you as an individual, but rather can be seen as something instilled in us from without.

So, it's really valuable to be able to silence these cultural fears, right?

Yes.

And no.

As we've already noted, if you want to be effective at creating material to speak to your culture, your world, those around you, you will need to be immersed in the world to such an extent that your work will relate to it and will be understood by the people. We've also noted that creativity is often a case of taking what is known and expected, and making it into something different. Reframing the known as the unknown. This requires knowing and being familiar with what is already expected. So, trying to create without a cultural context will be difficult to sell. And difficult to achieve because we all, always, have a cultural context. Furthermore, remember why we create? It's because things are unsettled, in a state of disequilibrium. The awareness of that disequilibrium will come from being aware of the culture you are seeking to 'equalise'. And here is the crux of the problem. That disequilibrium, that discomfort with the way things are, is exactly the point at which the fear will likely strike. My desire to creatively explore my understanding of indigenous cultures is going to clash with both the white belief I live in and the indigenous world I want to understand better. So I have two choices. Either;

One: Accept that I don't know enough, that I am not culturally or experientially capable of understanding indigenous culture and so I should just shut up and write about white men who mow their own lawns and watch football, things I do have the 'right' to express.

Or

Two: Know that I don't know about indigenous life and write about *that*, my own ignorance, fearlessly taking up things that may cause offence or be wrong, understanding that only by being wrong can I learn.

The problem is that even as I sit down to write what I hope will be a powerful, incisive exploration of my own white ignorance, I am constantly aware that I would be financially better off and more liked if I wrote a good fun book about lawn mowing and football. The difference is; lawn mowing and football don't cause me any great internal disequilibrium. And this indigenous writing thing is only this week's issue. Next week it might be something else. For all of us the cultural curses can be all sorts of other things. Parenting rules, childhood terrors, stupid decisions you'd rather forget, what you believe, what you chose to hate, songs that suck, and so on and on and on.

Knowing what it is that I fear, I am able to name it and face it. Some creators will decide to turn away from the things they fear and that's okay. Not everyone needs to give the world a kick. But if you do want to, you'll need to know how to fight against your own cultural curses to do it. So, as we get to the pointy end of the highly creative life, I offer you 3 very simple things to help you powerfully execute your creative gifts, staying true to yourself and striving to become even better at what you do.

It All Boils Down to This:

Who's got the Cultural Curse?

- Being your most creative self will most likely see you clash with your own fears.

- Your fears are frequently part of the culture that you live in, and no one wants to be rejected from their culture.

- No one really knows what culture is, that's why it's so hard to determine your place in it.

- Know why you back down from a creative choice and you may find the hidden fear.

- Your past has installed your fears, but also the knowledge you need to speak into your world. It is bad and good.

Brown, Tim. In *Great TED talks; creativity*. May, Tim. (ed) Portico. 2020

Koppett, Kat. *Training to Imagine : Practical Improvisational Theatre Techniques for Trainers and managers to Enhance Creativity, Teamwork, Leadership, and Learning*. Routledge. 2001

Lubart Todd I. and Georgsdottir, Asta. Creativity: Developmental and Cross-Cultural Issues. In *Creativity; when East meets West.* Sing Lau, et al. (Eds) World Scientific. 2004

Runco, Mark. Personal Creativity and Culture. In *Creativity; when East meets West.* Sing Lau, et al. (Eds) World Scientific. 2004

Rushdie, Salman. The Disappeared How the fatwa changed a writer's life. *The New Yorker* Sept. 17. 2012

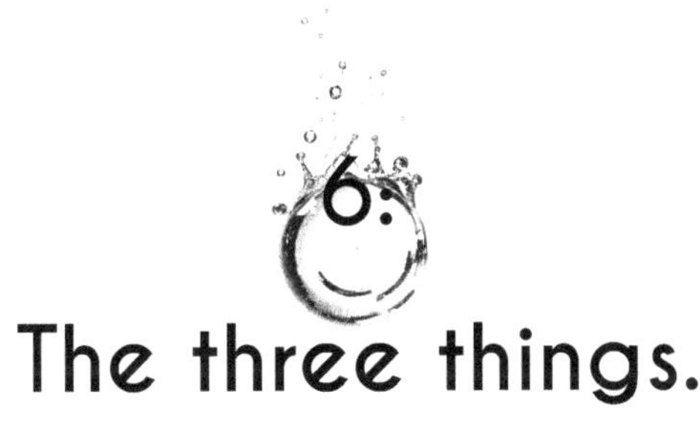

6: The three things.

Thing one:

Humble Be.

> Humility means a real attentiveness to the promise that is perhaps still lying some way beneath the surface, to be uncovered only if we sit quietly enough, listening hard. (luminous, 73)
>
> CHARLOTTE WOOD

Now that we've set the scene and looked at all the things that affect and effect your creativity; now that we all know what it is and why we do it, we can finally get to the fun bit. HOW.

If you have picked up this book and joined in here, welcome along, glad you could make it. You've missed a whole lot of interesting stuff that makes all of this make sense, but at least you're here for the next bits. And, if you find yourself thinking 'what the heck is this all about?' you can always go back and find out. The point is, getting better at being creative and getting sharper, smarter and more efficient at it, is exactly like creating something hugely excellent. It's a journey. It takes time. And it takes a lot of patience. And creating something, as we have already explored, means spending a lot of time 'wrong.' Wouldn't it be nice if there was an easy way to cope with all of this, to absorb the criticisms, the failings, the self-doubt of being a highly creative person?

Well, there is. Or there are. Three things to be exact. Three simple understandings that will make the journey so much easier. In fact, you probably already know them by now, from your own creative life and from the first five bits of this book. The three things that help a highly creative person survive and thrive. They are so simple and obvious you may need to be convinced of their efficacy. I shall endeavour to do exactly that and introduce more wisdom from those creative wonders in our world who epitomise these three things.

Starting with the first. A very simple trait that may look so wrong because, at first glance, most of the highly creative people you see kind of look completely the opposite.

Thing one to embrace as a highly thriving creative human being:

Be Humble.

For many of us this is a real problem. Not because we are tremendously arrogant but because we are tremendously good at putting ourselves down. Don't. Being humble is *not* about being put down. As you create and express your creativity there will be plenty of forces outside wanting to put you down. 'Reality' being just one. What really matters about creativity is probably more about picking yourself *up*. Reminding yourself of how valuable you and your creativity are. But more on that shortly.

There's a great understanding of true humility in the bible. Whether you believe in God or not, just sit with this idea a second. God says to people "Humble yourself before me and I will be your God." Simple enough but look at the complexity underlying it. We humans are to be humble before God. Why? Because God is God and we aren't. Man's biggest failing in the story of the bible is that we assume the place of God and try to be God. Humbling oneself means we put ourselves in the *right* position with the massive all knowing, all seeing, all everything, God of the universe. Okay? Bear with me, this is the cool bit. Why does God, the all everything of everything ask us to be humble? So we can be with God. Walk with God, talk with God and just... be. That's the picture we get from the garden of Eden. So, we humble ourselves by having... and here's the point... a true and authentic understanding of the sheer incredible power and worth of what we are being humble in front of. Now, instead of humbling yourself before God, because God is God and we're not, what happens if you see your creativity and its product as something amazing, incredible and intrinsically valuable? Can you boldly and bravely stand humbly in the light of what your brilliant human creativity can do? Notice that it is a choice. We can put ourselves in a humble place and draw huge benefits, as we'll see shortly. Or we can choose to *not* be humble, and cut ourselves off from some really powerful creative tools.

Humility is about the ability to have a realistic view of your work. Here's another way to think about your humility. Can you have a view of it that someone who is not you might have? You are invested, deeply absorbed and deeply passionate about the work. If you're not, you won't create it. As writing coach Janna Lopez has said,

> Words are self-expression. They are born from places within us that are part of who we are… With this in mind, when someone puts themselves out there to share their writing with me, what they're sharing is who they are. (14)

In an article on '*The courage to be different*,' in *New Philosopher* magazine, the point is made that 'Possibly controversial or novel ideas are best kept secret for fear of ridicule or bullying, or worse being silenced by those who once 'loved' or 'liked' them.' That means shutting up about what you've done, self-editing so you don't stand out. That's a massive killer of creativity. It is fear, as we mentioned in the previous chapter. Fear is not humility.

Fear is based on a misunderstanding of your value and the anxiety about being found out, among other things. Humility is a strength. It is about being so assured of your ability to finally create the worthwhile thing, that you are willing for other people to help you and work with you. You may even be happy for others to try and tear it down. Okay, that may sound a bit extreme, but, as you face the reality of sharing your work, face it like this.

Fear = weak = bad.

Humility = strength = good.

It sure as hell doesn't feel like it though, does it? Humility is scary. So, what's happening here?

Once your creative work is ready to be seen, humility allows you to run it through someone else's brain. For this to be valuable, it means preferencing the beliefs of others over your own. You are, in this moment, giving them more control than you give yourself. It's about being aware of your weaknesses and human failing, but not succumbing to it and not accepting it as the way things must be. Ernest Hemingway, in a letter to Ivan Kashkin, in 1935, wrote that,

> Writing is something that you can never do as well as it can be done. It is a perpetual challenge and it is more difficult than anything else that I have ever done- so I do it. And it makes me happy when I do it well. (Selected letters, 419)

Your work is very personal. It's yours. As we saw earlier, it even feels like it *is* you. Now, however, as you turn the work over to others, an editor, audience, viewer, it is in their hands. Your life is in their hands. Know that feeling? The thing about that feeling is that it's a good thing... and a bad thing. It's good because without that connection and passion you create nothing. It's bad because if you become *too* invested in the work, it takes over your life and then, if someone doesn't like it, you feel like they don't like you.

A quick reality check here. The fact is, some people are just not going to like you. Famous or not. In fact, the more people who know you, or know your work, the larger the number of people who don't like you. It's a simple fact of numbers. Put that aside and note the difference for the creator. If someone at work or in your school didn't like you that's one thing, but if someone doesn't like your creative work, well, now it's personal. And that hurts more. Weird huh? But wait, it gets worse. The person at school who called you 'stinky bum head', or whatever it was, the way around that is to ignore them. But if you have just released a book, artwork, song, film, whatever, and the things they are saying about you are all over the internet, what does the wise, highly effective creative do? They listen. They humbly and quietly assess the criticism to decide if it is valid. Okay, first you'll probably rage, curse and point to the ignorance of said critic. *Never* do this in public or online. Because the next step is *vital*. If there is some validity in their criticism that might make you and your created product better in the future, this is where you will hear it. The artist Jerry Salz notes that 'I always tell anyone criticizing me "you could be right." It has a nice double edge; Sometimes the victim never feels a thing' (104) You need to take a deep breath and, wearing your humblest sackcloth, listen to them. That's the best thing you can do. You don't have to like your critics, you certainly don't have to agree with them, but it is a good idea to listen to them. Even if they are wrong.

Charlotte Wood is a successful and critically acclaimed Australian novelist. But that doesn't happen by accident. She has been brave enough to splash her failings and understanding of her creative work across the pages of a book called The *Luminous Solution.* In it she says:

> With my own work in progress there always comes a time when I need a fellow writer's eyes upon it. For me that point is usually around three-quarters of the way towards a book's completion, when it's sturdy enough to withstand a good critical nudge without collapse, yet still malleable enough to allow substantial change. (70)

That right there is a picture of humble at work. Note well what she says. Who does she 'trust' with her heart and soul? A fellow writer. Someone who understands the journey and the process. Not a friend or a family member. And when does she do it? When the work is strong enough on its own to take some robust challenging.

The other side to this 'humble' thing is when we don't really know what we have or don't really 'own' it. If you listen to the novelist Haruki Murakami, he sounds like it's all a bit bewildering.

> I'm not intelligent. I'm not arrogant. I'm just like the people who read my books. I used to have a jazz club, and I made the cocktails and I made the sandwiches. I didn't want to become a writer—it just happened. It's a kind of gift, you know, from the heavens. So I think I should be very humble. (354)

One of Haruki Murakami's 'fans' is Michael Gallant who, in a blog article, made this point.

> I generally love books by Haruki Murakami, but I have friends who can't stand his writing… If you get less-than-ideal feedback on your writing, remember that a negative reaction simply means that your work didn't resonate with that individual reader; … Don't ignore negative

> reactions to your work — they can be far more valuable than hearing people gush over how amazing you are — but keep critical feedback in context. If someone doesn't like your work, learn what you can from the experience and keep writing.

With all that in mind, let me answer the question that is obvious to all. Why is 'humble' such a useful thing? Why do I need to be humble to thrive creatively? What is happening when I put my sense of self on hold and let someone else tell me what they think?

I think there are a couple of things happening here. The first, most obvious thing, we'll talk about a bit more later but it's kind of self-explanatory. It is this. Being humble means you are open to change from outside. You are accepting that your work, your idea, whatever, may not be perfect and may need some changing. We looked earlier at living with 'wrong' in your work. This is how you act that out. The ability to sit with 'wrong' in your work and let it grow, is a vital part of the work becoming excellent. Taking the flash and whoosh of the creative flow state and now, making it subservient to the executive control of the wiser creative part of you, needs to be done in this humble place. Partly, this goes back to the understanding that the 'flow' you isn't the best one to finally edit, frame or even promote your work. You need to hand it over to the more reasoned, logical part of your creative self. And that's an act of humbling. It touches on everything we have mentioned so far.

Eric Grierson wrote about *The Certainty Trap,* in which he explored the psychological concept of *Intellectual Humility.* Or, for the real world, let's just call it 'humility'. He notes that Intellectual Humility is;

> "the degree to which one accepts that they could be wrong"- and that someone who's challenging their position could be right, or at least more right than they're giving them credit for. (40)

Humility lets you take on board differences of opinion. Certainly, this means you need to be aware of who you are humbling yourself *to.* Is this person actually a good judge? Should you 'give them credit' for their opinion? And so on. Being humble about your work doesn't mean assuming that your work is rubbish, that you are rubbish, or that it's all a waste of time. It means having a balanced view of yourself and your work. I am capable, I am valuable in this domain, and this work is worthwhile. But it can be better. Kind of like saying to yourself 'Damn that's good. But is it *really* good?' Then, the humble creative will ask 'who knows?' Eric Grierson mentions that researchers in the field 'have found that people high in [Intellectual Humility] are even interested in understanding the reasons that people disagree with them'. (42) So it goes beyond

'Can this be better,' to being humble enough to ask '*how* will your opinion make a huge difference?'

This aspect of humility, the desire to take on another viewpoint, and the willingness to be curious about how and why your creative work is the way it is, may be far more central than we assume. Shortly we will dive deeper into how much power there is in simply being curious, but for now, I want to suggest there is also great creative power in community.

I know, as a writer of stories, I hate having my work seen by people before it's 'ready'. Whatever that means. I hate sitting in the same room with someone reading my work. Snakes, spiders, I'd rather sit with them. There is something profoundly unsettling for me to be there whilst my creative soul is bared to another. Do you know what I mean? I'm happy for it to appear in newspapers, blog-up on the web and I love people buying my novels. Just don't read them in front of me. Now, however, I lecture in creative writing and every class includes a time of writing something and then sharing it. I instruct students to write, and read their work to the class and so I do it too. Strangely, I don't find this as traumatic. Why? Perhaps because we're all in the same boat. I learn enormously from my fellow writers and in this class situation we have all written on a level playing field. We have written in community. The profound value of this didn't strike me until I was delving into the music creating process and came across research that pointed out that;

> In performing creatively, ensemble musicians face two primary challenges: generating original (but stylistically appropriate) ideas and maintaining co-ordination while translating these ideas into musical output (4)

Laura Bishop's work highlights the incredible value of highly skilled musicians working together, shaping each other's output and creating this amazing dance of pure creative invention whilst, at the same time, remaining within the requirements of the music they are reading from. It is the perfect example of flow and executive control being active at the same time. Imagine your favourite music, played by people with domain excellence, live and passionate and in person. Pure creativity. Pure rock n roll. But humble?

Laura Bishop speaks of the 'embodied music cognition' (EMC) paradigm [that] conceptualizes cognition as distributed between a person's brain, body, and environment. (Bishop, 3) In other words, this joyful, powerful, unified, performance of individuals becoming a singular creative musical entity can only come about because the value of their personal skill and experience, brain and body, is matched to their environment, those working with them and even the audience. And that means no single performer in this group can be the controller. Even though there may be a star on stage, each part of the group is in control and can also alter the rest of the group.

So was Michael Jackson humble? John Lennon? Katie Perry? Well, I never played with them but if you see them sound-checking, yes, perhaps they were. Brilliantly domain excellent but also completely aware of the need for others and their need to work with them.

I have come to the understanding that as a novelist, I can't afford to just write a book. I need help to create a symphony. I bring the literary music and I humbly ask others to join me in bringing my literary music to life. Just to finish with this music creativity picture for the moment, I think Laura Bishop makes a powerful point when she explains how this creative community creates something amazing. She notes that; 'it occurs when a group performs in a way that cannot be attributed to any one individual contributor.' (9) Surely this can apply to actors working with directors and special effects people; authors working with cover designers and editors. Are sporting teams or even individual sports stars anything without coaches, physios and so on? All of us need a community to create powerfully and an arrogant person quickly finds themselves alone. The humble creator will live in a close-knit community of passionate support.

Here's a thought for you: In a piece titled "The Many Faces of Creativity", Shulamith Kreitler suggests that 'Creativity is often considered as a major resource of development, well-being, change, and growth for individuals and societies. Some consider it even as humankind's ultimate resource' (4) But maybe creativity can be seen as a core component of community? And community may be a core component of creativity?

As strange as it may seem at first, humble is a very powerful tool for the highly creative individual. It allows you to take on advice, to use the knowledge and viewpoint of those you trust, and to be constantly changing your created stuff to make it better and better. Being humble allows you to live in a supportive creative community. When explaining how improvisational theatre teams work together, Kat Koppet finds that the creative space can be easily broken but also is capable of supporting great success.

> The only way to maximize creative risk is to celebrate the brave failure as well as the triumphant success. If failure is punished, then the risk of risking is just too high. Of course, there are times when following an innovative path will result in defeat. That defeat must be acknowledged and valued as a necessary cost of

> implementing the right process, or the process will be discarded with the result. (27)

That is a picture of community, of support, of working together. It also requires humility from all. So 'be humble and you will create fearlessly'?

Yes.

And No.

When Margaret Boden wrote her book on the creative brain, she landed upon this:

> Creativity does not come cheap. Sometimes it comes at a very high cost indeed… This commitment involves not only passionate interest, but self-confidence too. A person needs a healthy self-respect to pursue novel ideas, and to make mistakes, despite criticism from others. Self-doubt there may be, but it cannot always win the day. Breaking generally accepted rules, or even stretching them, takes confidence. Continuing to do so, in the face of scepticism and scorn, takes even more. (255)

I would say it takes community. Others supporting your passion because you are worth it. And a sense that you are part of something bigger. You're not doing this alone. Something to remember about all created work is this. It is edited. It is produced. It is refined. Even when presented live, the work of an artist is rarely, if ever, just thrown out there.

A stand-up comedian, working seemingly off the top of their head, is simply drawing on pages and pages of notes or ideas that they filed away for just this time. Usually, they are ideas they have already tested on their friends. Watch a stand up at work and you will see the pause, the rest, as the joke lands or they just walk the stage examining the audience. This is not simply a matter of timing. It is a time for the performer to flip through the notes in their head and pick the right piece for right now. They are not at rest, they are at work, examining all the material they have already created and tried out earlier. Perhaps there is no greater pain than being best mates with a novice comedian and having to suffer their endless practice. Like being the parent of a beginner saxophonist. They need all the help they can get. And this is how it works in practice. This is what the humble writer can do with a bit of humble editing. A published book for example, will not just be the authors voice and story. It will be a polished, refined, hopefully perfected version of their voice and work. Novelist and writing coach Harry Birmingham points to how;

> the repetitious action of read/react/change/re-read ends up building into something that is you, but is also bigger

> than you. More humane. Funnier. More observant. More insightful. More nuanced. More coherent.

Surely that's how it should be? The best 'you' on the page, on the stage, hanging on the wall? Perfected through humble, communal, creative correction.

If you find you have written a book that everyone praises and fawns over, it's not a bad idea to do two things so you can remain humble, but correctly humble.

One: Recognise that you are a writer who can do that, but you can't do it alone.

Two: recognise that it was nowhere near as easy as it looks to someone reading your work. Or, again in the words of Ernest Hemingway, who could write pretty well;

> I love to write. But it has never gotten any easier to do and you can't expect it to if you keep trying for something better than you can do. (Selected letters, 893)

In his autobiography Bono talks about the process of creating the world spanning songs for which U2 are famous. It's not likely many people see the humility in Bono, because he is a huge star who ignites the world's biggest stadiums just by standing on stage and sharing his songs. But that's his job. His gift. The talent he shares, refined, defined, edited and shaped to its final product. In this process, Bono points to this ability to let go of the self in the face of criticism. He says that:

> Suspension of disbelief is not just critical for appreciation of an artwork; it's necessary for its manufacture. It's not about rolling your eyes when something goes wrong, as if to say "I told you we shouldn't be here." (263)

Or, to put it another way, Antonia Case writes about *Befriending Fear* and notes the inevitability of fear, the one thing guaranteed to kill your creativity. Bono overcomes fear of failure by 'suspending disbelief', and it's a really helpful insight, in light of what Antonia notes:

> Complete certainty, safety, and a life of no fear is impossible. There'll never be a point in your life where you'll think, "now's the right time, I'm totally prepared and at ease..." If you wait for the fear to go away first, you'll never do it. Because the fear is never going away. (Case)

Waiting for the time to be right means waiting for ever. Achieving nothing. Creating only emptiness. Self-confidence helps you to make. The humility to examine your creation helps you re-make it into something greater than you can ever make on your own. And the underlying power of humility here, have you seen it? All the criticism you get, all the opposing views?

Who is in control of them? You are. The creator. It is *your* creativity that will ultimately decide what goes forward. It's like you have a map and are driving somewhere you've never been before. You can follow the map or you can ignore it. Both can be useful. Remember when GPS was first around? I remember once driving down to the port in an area I had never been.

> 'In one hundred meters continue straight on.'

I ignored the suggestion because there was a massive river in the way. To follow this supposedly wise, all-knowing technology would have turned my car into a submarine. To blindly trust the voice of others can be fatal. Self-confidence is vital. The final decision, the power of the work, is yours and yours alone. But it's best when it's yours alone, in a community.

When your work starts getting into the world you will need to find the balance within yourself. I've had a similar conversation with pretty much every author I know, when the publisher starts throwing edits, corrections and suggestions at them. 'I don't want to change that, why are they making this change? What is wrong with that? I don't like their suggestion, what should I do?' The answer is always the same. You don't have to listen to your publisher or editor. It is your work, your creative output. You control it. But they don't have to publish your work. So listen, understand why they want the changes and then make a decision. Without humility, you won't even listen.

My colleague, novelist J.A. Cooper says he has three levels of editing consideration when he is humbly sitting in front of pages of edits from his publisher. He must decide if the suggested change is;

A: Vital. This is wrong or breaks the story. The publisher is insisting on the edit.

B: Probable. This edit is a good idea, it flows better, makes more sense or corrects a minor error.

C: Possible. The editor thinks this is better but it's not a deal breaker, it's up to you…

He then decides if these edits will be committed to the final work. If it's in the 'A' category, and he disagrees with the edit, he knows this may sink the publication. If it's in the 'C' category, no-one is going to lose sleep over it. The thing is, the publisher might not point out which edits are deal breakers and which aren't, until later. He has to know what he's doing and, more importantly, who he is working with and whether he trusts their opinion as much as his own. Can he be humble? That same humility applies to all processes. Song making, creating a business concept, talking on the radio, presenting television weather, whatever. Can you be the star, and be humble?

Another thing to note here is how this question of being humble and having a true and valuable understanding of your own creative skill and power, can directly impact your ability to create. I've met many people who say 'I'm just not that creative.'

As we noted earlier, they are absolutely right. But it's mainly because they have already decided they aren't. Yet, after talking a while, I can point to a number of areas where they feel they have skill and talent and are, quite obviously, creative. They just don't see it like that because 'I'm not that creative.'

Sigh.

The problem here is that this downplaying of the innate and natural creativity in all of us shuts down the engine that drives it. We think we can't fly free with the creative eagles so we waddle like ducks. Or, as Mikhalyi Csikszentmihalyi notes in his seminal work on flow:

> A less drastic obstacle to experiencing flow is excessive self-consciousness. A person who is constantly worried about how others will perceive her, who is afraid of creating the wrong impression, or of doing something inappropriate, is also condemned to permanent exclusion from enjoyment. So are people who are excessively self-centered. A self-centered individual is usually not self-conscious, but instead evaluates every bit of information only in terms of how it relates to her desires. (84)

Notice how much 'self' understanding is related to being able to enjoy the creative flow state? But self-confidence is not included as a negative. Held in balance, self-confidence and humility unleash the creative forces within. I know I am good enough to do this. Plus, I know I will need others to help me make it the best it can be. I am good enough. With help. Perhaps it's time to present a useful definition of how you, the highly creative individual, can understand humility.

Humility. The ability, the art, of knowing that although you are highly skilled, you always have things to learn and you are open to learning them.

I fight to get to this point. I try to believe that what I have created is the best I can do… but I'm willing, no, I'm *excited* to have it improved by others.

In your understanding of creative people you know, is this what you see?

This *does not* mean you constantly put yourself down. But it does mean that just because you are the creator, the novelist, the band leader, the painter, the designer, that you know everything, that your work can't be improved with a bit of outside observation. Here, your curiosity needs to kick in.

To thrive creatively there must be a clear understanding of the two things required of your self-image. That you are unique, amazing, created to be brilliant. And two… you need others, you are *not* perfect. You fail often. Both are true. Both are central to your creative gift. Be brilliant. And be humble. I love this quote from Jeff and Julia Crabtree's handbook to *Living with a creative mind.*

> A man should carry two stones in his pocket. On one should be inscribed: "I am but dust and ashes". And on the other: "For my sake was the world created," and he should use each as one has need.
>
> (A rabbi, 172)

It All Boils Down to This:

Being humble

- Creativity requires community, the input of others, to become a valuable product.

- You never know what you don't know. So you need to appreciate the ideas of others as much as your own.

- Being humble is *not* putting yourself down. It is knowing how good you are and how good others can help you become.

- Humility means letting others into your creative work. It does *not* mean handing it over completely. The humble creative remains wisely in control.

- Humility allows your work to be imperfect, and to keep pushing it to be better.

Bateson, Patrick, and Martin, Paul. *Play, Playfulness, Creativity and Innovation*. Cambridge, 2013

Birmingham, Harry. The fourth line and then the fifth. *Jericho writers*. https://community.jerichowriters.com/page/view-post?id=308

Bishop, Laura. Collaborative Musical Creativity: How Ensembles Coordinate Spontaneity. In *Frontiers in Psychology*. Vol 9, Article 1285. July. 2018

Boden, Margaret. *The Creative Mind*. Cardinal books. 1992

Bono. *Surrender*. Hutchinson. 2021

Case, Antonia. Befriending fear. in *New Philosopher*. p 22. Nov. 2022

Crabtree, Jeff and Julia. *Living with a creative Mind*. Zebra Collective. 2011

Csikszentmihalyi, Mihaly. *Flow. The Psychology of optimal experience*. Harper Collins. 1990

Michael Gallant. How To Deal With Writing Criticism And Negative Feedback. https://blog.bookbaby.com/how-to-write/writing-inspiration/writing-criticism February 4. 2023

Grierson, Eric. The Certainty Trap. In *Psychology Today*. Vol 56 No 4. Pp 38-44. August. 2023

Hemingway, Ernest. *Ernest Hemingway: The last interview and other conversations*. Melville house. 2015

Koppett, Kat. *Training to Imagine: Practical Improvisational Theatre Techniques for Trainers and Managers to Enhance Creativity, Teamwork, Leadership, and Learning*. Routledge. 2001

Kreitler, Shulamith. The Many Faces of Creativity by way of Introduction. In *New Frontiers in Creativity*. Shulamith Kreitler (ed) Nova science. 2020

Lopez, Janna. Choose Kindness When You Give Writing Feedback. https://blog.bookbaby.com/how-to-write/good-writing-habits/writing-feedback February 1. 2023

Murakami, Hyuki. *Paris Review interviews IV,* The Paris Review. 2009

Woods, Charlotte. *The Luminous solution.* Allen and Unwin. 2021

The courage to be different. *New Philosopher.* p 14. Nov. 2022

A word about...
Creating and listening to music.

Creativity, like life itself, is constantly throwing things at me. Just when I think I'm getting a handle on it, the handle comes off and the whole thing falls back onto the baggage carousel for another go around. As part of the summer school sessions this year I had students across the country joining me on-line to share our understandings of the course I presented. These tutorials included workshops in which one student would present a simple 'task' and we would perform it and then discuss what this task showed us about our creativity. These workshops, in the hands of students asking questions, have been a constant source of me dropping the luggage and having to look at things again. Here's one from Coralie, a schoolteacher, musician and carer, who took on the study to help herself find her creative space. In doing so she threw open a whole new understanding of how I create and how many I know find struggle in the process. Let me start at the beginning.

On a warm Tuesday evening, I was in my office. One of the students was in his car driving across New South Wales, another student was in her own office. Coralie was in Queensland. Coralie gave us this creative challenge.

She played different music pieces for thirty seconds each and had us write down images, inspirations, things that came to mind. There was mellow acoustic, some funky jazz and a piece of glittering praise. Try it, it's a good experiment. What we came to was this question: Does the presence of music have the effect of 'cognitive dampening', engaging an element of the cognitive process in something non-essential and allowing the creative effort to flow undistracted by the background of life?

We talked about it and decided that for musicians this will be very different as the background distraction *is* the creative domain they are working in. Also, for musicians, do they attend more to the background music when performing other tasks (*Like the Alternative Uses Task*) than non-musicians who can just let it be since it is not their creative domain?

Is there a difference in attention and freeing of the mind between known and unknown music in the background?

Is this kind of like TENS (Transitory Electric Nerve Stimulus) for the brain? In TENS a tiny electric pulse is sent along a nerve pathway to block it from expressing pain, thereby providing a painless and momentary analgesia. Sort of. Is this a good physical analogue of the cognitive work going on here? Does giving our brain a little something to chew on in 'the background,' free up the brain for harder cognitive work? There is even a thing called 'The Mozart effect', which suggests that *'people perform better on tests of spatial abilities after listening to music composed by Mozart.' (Thompson et al, 248)* But the suggestion is that something in the music itself is at work. Thompson's people found that; *Participants performed better on a test of spatial abilities after listening to a Mozart sonata than after sitting in silence. (Thompson et al. 250)*

So there may be something about the music itself, but something also about what our neurons and thoughts are doing. But what? I don't know, and the class didn't have an agreed position, because some of us like a bit of background music, some don't. And for many people it's a sometimes thing. I like writing in a crowded noisy place, others hate it. The underlying question is 'what happens in that place? What is the noise doing for *you?'*

A recent study found pretty much what we found in class, but put it like this:

> *Our findings showed that when compared to a quiet environment, both instrumental and vocal music as background stimuli significantly affected AUT* [Creativity task] *performance. Notably, music with a negative emotional charge bolstered individual originality in creative performance. These results lend support to the dual role of background music in creativity, with instrumental music appearing to enhance creativity through factors such as emotional arousal, cognitive interference, music preference, and psychological restoration. (Xiao et al, 01)*

There are whole books written on the uses and effects of music in life, so I won't bang on about it here, except to make this observation. What is going on in the 'background' as you create can have a huge impact on how you do it. If you can control your environment, you can control that impact. And it's worth finding what things dampen the internal interference for you.

Xiao X, Tan J, Liu X and Zheng M. The dual effect of background music on creativity: perspectives of music preference and cognitive interference. *Frontiers in Psychology*. 14:1247133. doi: 10.3389/fpsyg.2023.1247133. 2023

Thompson, W. F., Glennschellenberg, E., and Husain, G. Arousal, mood, and the Mozart effect. *Psychol. Sci.* 12, 248–251. doi: 10.1111/1467-9280.00345. 2001

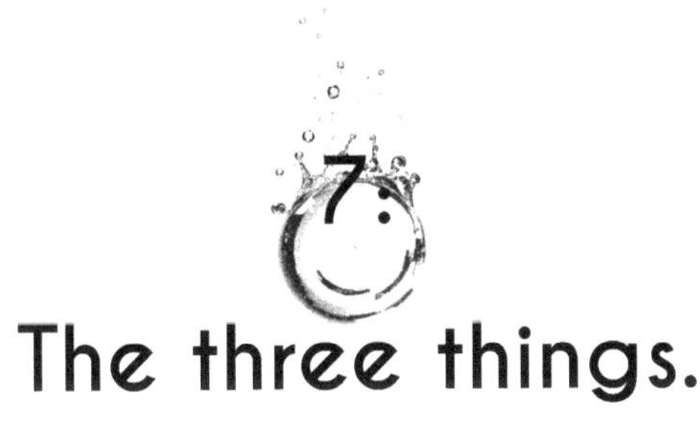

7: The three things.

Thing Two:

Being a curious child.

> Rather than regarding play as what the child does, the better way is to focus on play as an internal disposition to be playful. (319)
>
> LYNN BARNETT

I am now happy with humility, the first thing I need to thrive as a highly effective creative person. It's good to know I'm good at what I do, but it's great to get others involved and helping. Humbly being a valuable part of a communal relationship, bringing creativity to the world and all that. Okay, I'm still working on it, but I know what I need to aim for. It's a journey and I'm on my way. Now it's time to look at how I can take my existing creative power and crank it right up. Let me share with you, the pure creative power of not growing up.

First thing to do is realise that this doesn't feel right, does it? For a long time, we have been culturally shaped to not be children. The world wants you to grow up. It's what parents, teachers, and criminal court judges, will all tell you. Grow up. Stop mucking about. Stop being so childish. *'Get a haircut and get a real job'* (Thorogood) to quote the song.

This is not a new thing. Even as long ago as the bible, there has been the call to stop being such a child. The Apostle Paul was writing a letter to a bunch of people in the city of Corinth. That letter is in the bible, and in it, Paul tells the people 'When I was a child, I talked like a child, I thought like a child, I reasoned like a child. When I became a man, I put the ways of childhood behind me.' (1 Corinthians, 13:11)

Or, to paraphrase: It's time to grow up and stop being such children.

Sorry Paul the Apostle, I'm about to tell everyone to do the exact opposite. But that's okay because the Bible actually says that, too. When Matthew is telling his story, he mentions that Jesus himself told people, "Let the little children come to me, and do not hinder them, for the kingdom of heaven belongs to such as these." (Matthew 19:14)

So not only is it good to be a child, according to Jesus, but he tells everyone that the kingdom of heaven belongs to children. And that sounds like a good thing.

Is the bible is contradicting itself? Well, maybe. But this is not a theological discussion, it's about the reality of your creativity and my suggestion that you need to behave like a child. In creativity, we find that the same contradiction exists powerfully. Is this a surprise?

It feels like playing and being creative are kind of linked, but because we're also expected to live in a world of adults and grownups, playing is often frowned upon, seen as frivolous or a waste of time. Even dangerous.

Sandra Russ did some research looking at pretend play, that is imaginary making-stuff-up kind of play. She notes that;

> there is strong evidence that processes expressed in pretend play are associated with measures of creativity, especially with divergent thinking. There is some evidence from longitudinal studies that this association is stable over time. Converging evidence suggests that cognitive and affective processes in pretend play are involved in adult creative production. (21)

In other words, people who can pretend can create. And they started as kids but keep going as adults.

To put this in perspective, let me lean on one of the definitions of creativity from Robert Weisberg. He says, 'Creative thinking is ordinary thinking plus expertise.' (245)

The point here is that creativity is successfully expressed through expertise. What we can call Domain Excellence. Skill. Experience. This is pretty logical. The better you are at the skill, art, talent, science, whatever, the better your creative process can shine. Like a tennis player, training for years long before they make it to centre court. The hours of relentless practice a guitarist puts in before they can take their debut single into the studio or onto the stage. You know the story. Creativity comes from hours and hours of hard work building excellence. This is the one thing a child can never have. Let's just take that on-board for the moment as one side of the seesaw. Half of the balance. Being creative, being highly successful as a creative person involves knowing your stuff and getting better at it. This will never end. Many people now espouse the value of life-long learning. If you don't already know why that is such a huge thing, stick around, it's about to make a lot of sense. Being powerful in your domain, being good at your art, from sketching to surgery, from astronauts to authors, skill is a vital component of your success.

But that's only one side.

The problem is that this side of the balance is measurable, identifiable, and visible. Skill, outcomes, the product of your work, learning, developing, increasing your domain excellence, becoming more expert; these can be measured, and even given a grade or a degree or a gold star. Therefore, the way to become 'better' in your domain looks like it's all about learning, growing, becoming more expert. Adult stuff. Because that is what is measured and held up to the light.

But what we don't see is the other side, the balance. The *other* thing you need to grow as a highly effective creative human being. I'm talking about;

Being a child.

Jean Piaget, developmental psychologist and historically relevant thinker on child development, notes two very important things about creativity that much research since has supported. Creativity is innate and it gets crushed out of us. He apparently said that:

> if you want to be creative stay in part a child, with the creativity and invention that characterizes children before they are deformed by adult society.

So, one reason we lose our creativity is because we become 'deformed by adult society?' Perhaps. Hold that thought.

Steven Levitt and Stephen Dubner have become famous in recent years for developing the concept of *Freakanomics*, the book, podcast and T-shirt in which "A Rogue Economist Explores the Hidden Side of Everything." In their book *Think like a freak*, they suggest this:

> When it comes to generating ideas and asking questions, it can be really fruitful to have the mentality of an eight year old... Kids are...relentlessly curious and relatively unbiased. Because they know so little, they don't carry around the preconceptions that often stop people from seeing things as they are... Kids are not afraid to share their wildest ideas. (87, 88)

This is a powerful understanding of creativity and its methodology that gets lost in all the hype, all the chatter and all the outside-looking-in misunderstanding. One problem is science itself. In its desire to understand 'play,' research has almost always ended up looking at the value of it. Again, I point you to the truth that what is measurable gets managed, so research into play will get funded if it is seeking to increase productivity. Therefore, pretty much all the research into play focuses on play as child development, child learning, or therapy. But there is a far deeper thing going on here, a power for all humans to enjoy. In a book called *For Want of Ambiguity: Order and Chaos in Art, Psychoanalysis, and Neuroscience,* Judovica Lumer notes that, 'Like the experience of emotion, play is a function of our most ancient brain regions and therefore to be viewed from a Darwinian perspective.' (36)

Or, if you prefer a creationist perspective, we play because our creator played. (Did God play? That's a whole other discussion but let me just say, have you ever *seen* a Platypus?) The point is, play seems to be ingrained, fundamental and foundational to the way the brain operates. Not just for children, but for all humans. As yet, however, there is no clear explanation of why and how. Jo Tyler recently wrote a chapter entitled "What really Happens when adults play." She says:

> We are convinced, intuitively and experientially, about the value of play. However, our confidence in the efficacy of play seems not to be matched by clear insights into why and how play actually achieves results. (1)

So, bottom line; what science, research, all the study, has come to is this; Play is good. It makes creativity good. Play is good for kids. Play is good for adults. But we don't know why. Or how. Perhaps we can sneak up on it sideways and look at play like this:

Let's imagine that there are things that define a highly creative individual. Which there are. And let's consider how these things, coincidentally, also define childlike play:

Highly effective creative people, and children:

They are Humble. Correctly humble. (not self-demeaning, but truly aware of their ability and their need for others.)

They are Curious. Deeply curious.

They are good with failure and ambiguity.

Yes, these are the 'Three things' were looking at and we've already touched on them a bit but let me now show you how we get more creative and more childlike in the face of failure and ambiguity.

If you're a manager or you're the boss and everyone is looking to you for guidance, or you are the breadwinner who must make the money and make the decisions, is being childlike an aspect of being the highly creative person you can deal with? I think this truth about being a child is best expressed by Sir Ken Robinson in his Ted talk "Do schools kill creativity?"

If you're not prepared to be wrong, you'll never come up with anything original. (2006)

This really hits home when you reframe it for your own professional space:

As a teacher am I okay being wrong in class?

As a pastor can I get it wrong in a sermon?

As a designer can I get an element wrong?

As a chef can I make a dodgy meal?

As a company manager, can I accept that I will get decisions wrong?

Just think about that for a minute because it's really vital to not just unleashing your creative self, but also to being a stable, powerful human. If you can't deal simply and humbly with your mistakes, every slip or potential error you make will knock you over. And the *fear* of getting knocked over will freeze you. As we know, one opposite of creativity is fear.

So how does this ambiguity, curiosity and child-like humility make you more successful creatively?

For most of us in the creative arts, 'wrong' can be something that seems unpopular, something that doesn't make sense, or doesn't fit. Something that is too different. This can be a matter of being the wrong thing for the wrong time, like a new type of music that doesn't fit. Yet. Or creating something that you have yet to polish (Any written work that has yet to be edited is wrong). We'll look at this in a bit more detail in the next bit. For now, notice that both of these 'Wrongs' occur and both are vital to creating powerful work. As we've already seen, the most exciting creative work pushes beyond boundaries, is therefore 'wrong', and needs time to be refined. Therefore, it spends time being wrong. Kelley and Kelley note the place of failure and being wrong in their book *Creative Confidence;*

> A widely held myth suggests that creative geniuses rarely fail… (However) Creative Geniuses, from artists like Mozart to scientists like Darwin, are quite prolific when it comes to failure- "Strokes of Genius" don't come about because they succeed more often than other people – they just DO more, period. (40)

How many times was *Harry Potter* rejected before he became a famous boy wizard? This being wrongness is often what kills our creative pursuit. We can safely make something like everyone else does; or we can push on, bend it, amp it, make it more unique, and thus make something new. *But* it will be a risk; There are risks to being highly creative and children don't care about those risks. Or, at least, they don't let the risks stop them. Or, even more likely, they don't *know* the risks deeply enough to fear them.

Can you imagine what your life might be like if you had no fear?

Alexander Fleming, who discovered penicillin, was famous for his playfulness. He was described, disapprovingly, by his boss as treating research like a game and finding it all great fun. When asked what he did, Fleming said 'I play with microbes ... it is very pleasant to break the rules and to be able to find something that nobody had thought of.' (In Bateson, 72)

Kary Mullis, who picked up the1993 Nobel prize for his creation of Polymerase Chain Reaction (PCR) which has changed the way we use DNA, has said 'I think really good science doesn't come from hard work. The striking advances come from people on the fringes, being playful.' (Case, intelligence, 22)

We can benefit by being childlike, experienced, highly productive, dreamers... which may seem totally contrary. Childlike *and* experienced? Have you ever seen a five-year-old complete a highly productive task? How do we juggle these contrary views in our heads without exploding?

If you look closely, you can probably find a swinging between extremes in all areas of your life. These are quite normal and quite helpful. It's how we have been designed. As those bible passages earlier noted. Be an adult and be a child. We are called to be humble and to know we are God's personal handcrafted children. We are created to be deeply curious and to have an unshakeable faith in things we don't yet know. As children there is a bonus. They don't know what they don't know, and they don't mind. But I'm a grown adult, I have a problem in that I know too much. You see, *just* having domain excellence, *only* becoming good at your thing can leave you stuck:

> the negative side of acquiring substantial knowledge on a topic is that it can lead to rigid, "fossilized" thinking. (Lubart, 29)

We all know this, probably in someone you have worked with. The most common expression is probably; "If all you have is a hammer, every problem looks like a nail."

If you look at the world of commercial radio, my former career, you'll notice there is nothing new. It is all the same, all predictable and every radio station does the same stuff.

Creativity is mostly dead. Fossilised. Why? Because the passionate, creative radio people who once ran the business have been pushed aside by the accountants and number managers, so the entire industry uses the same methods and measures to create the same thing.

The measurable is what is managed.

Numbers and costs.

Commercial TV is the same. Even Hollywood movies and 'popular' novels and music are in the same boat. Producers, publishers, gatekeepers, measure what worked in the past and assess the value of what the future can bring and decide on the thing that will most likely bring the most benefit. And by benefit, I mean money. Managers pursue what they can measure at the expense of what they can't manage. Childlike curiosity and humility and the ability to be wrong is not measurable and so it is… gone.

Does that make sense? Can you see this in your own world? Anyone who has worked in childcare, aged care, any government organisation, heck, pretty much anywhere, knows that the rules, regulations and restrictions that keep the bottom line safe and measurable are all that matters. In my local area, teachers of young children are now forbidden from hugging a distressed child. It's too legally risky. Thank you measurables for making modern childhood just another product.

Sigh. Okay, before I get all cynical and jaded, let's find a solution.

How can you become a new and more expanded, more engaged, more childlike, more wide-eyed you?

Play.

Have a mind that plays. Let your brain go and be a kid again. A lot! Patrick Bateson and his colleagues wrote a book about play as a powerful thing for adults. Interestingly, like every other play researcher he is focused on getting some value from play.

> The essence of our argument is that playful behaviour and playful thought can generate radically new approaches to challenges set by the physical and social environment. While our approach grew out of observations of non-human animals by biologists, we argue that humans and organisations can exploit playfulness as a tool for fostering creativity and innovation. (Bateson, 15)

They want to understand play as a device for creating more value. But let's look at what Bateson actually means by play: This is what they say makes meaningful, powerful productive play:

*** the behaviour is spontaneous and rewarding to the individual**

[Hitting a ball against a wall, doodling, daydreaming.]

*** it is intrinsically motivated and its performance is a goal in itself**

[you're not achieving anything more than the act. And the act is why you're doing it.]

*** the behaviour occurs in a protected context when the player is neither ill nor stressed.**

[So you might have to go to work with a monster headache, but you're not likely to be doodling.]

*** the behaviour is incomplete or exaggerated relative to non-playful behaviour in adults.**

[Hitting a ball against a wall is not a tennis match.]

*** it is performed repeatedly.**

(Bateson, 16)

Notice, this work from Patrick Bateson and his crew started as an exploration of how to arrive at creative solutions, how to make us more creative for the purpose of creating 'something' of extrinsic value, but what it comes down to is playing for its own sake.

And Play doesn't *have* to be what you *do*, it can be what you *are*. To be one who is playful...

Uninhibited.

Madeleine L'Engle, who created amazing stories like *A Wrinkle in Time,* says that, 'Children still haven't closed all their doors and all their windows. They're not afraid to get upset, and they're not afraid of new ideas. (259) And Maurice Sendak who gave us *Where the Wild Things Are,* said that children 'move between reality and fantasy with the greatest possible ease, without making categorical, specified lines where one stops and the other begins.' (23)

Why is this childlike mind set-so important to unleashing your creativity?

Well, obviously, if you are trying to be a being who brings new things into the world, and yet you are a being who relies on never offending the culture, or some image of what is right and acceptable, will you ever be free to create or will you be constantly checking and regulating yourself. Do you insist on those 'categorical, specified lines' between fantasy and reality that Maurice Sendak notes? Maybe without even noticing them? Do you 'check' your doodles? Do you keep score when you're hitting a ball against the wall?

The child allows all things in and discounts nothing. Their curiosity is fearless and free of form and boundaries. It's all wonderful, a confused mayhem of ideas flying in and out. And this is where we run into another very evident element of the highly creative person. You will almost always find that they are very curious.

Relentlessly Curious.

Roald Dahl, the man who gave us Charlie's chocolate factory, giant peaches and so many other wonderful flights of fancy, alluded to his relentless curiosity in an interview.

> Q: Many of your short story characters were collectors of one kind or another, people with very particular tastes...
>
> A: Yes, I suppose that's because I'm enormously interested in a number of things and have a fair knowledge of pictures, furniture, wines, etcetera. They are all things I love. So I make use of them. It's no good writing about things you don't know about. That's basic. Greyhound racing was another of my loves. I used to breed racing greyhounds. I knew about them so I wrote about them. (Dahl, 107)

I've mentioned that playing sport and being highly creative have many things in common. Curiosity is another one. In fact, Sara Santos and her colleagues believe sport is a great way to further enhance creativity across the board. They suggest that getting lost in a sport helps you to unleash your creative self. They find that;

> creative players require both the knowledge of a particular domain and that of cross domains. A broad knowledge in several domains may lead to a higher output of major innovations, thus making lasting contributions to their specific domain. (Santos, 361)

Knowing about things outside of their domains, being curious about the world beyond their expertise, made people more effective creatively within their domain. Hollywood producer and movie making legend Brian Grazer is passionately committed to curiosity. His book *A Curious Mind: The Secret to a Bigger Life* is a compelling tale of creativity powered by relentless, deliberate curiosity. He says:

> Curiosity has been the most valuable quality, the most important resource, the central motivation of my life. I think curiosity should be as much a part of our culture, our educational system, our workplaces, as concepts like "creativity" and "innovation". (xiii)

We've already noticed that Play, just playing, is a huge benefit in itself. So is curiosity. Just being curious is a powerful way of being. But it also feeds directly into the creative flow. Blues legend Skip James touches on the reality of how curiosity can become creativity. He put it like this:

> I've had quite an experience at different ages and different times. And that's the best teacher I found. That's something they cannot take away from you. Personal experience. (in Guralnick, 48)

For the person wanting to be highly creative, notice what happens. As you explore or pay attention to things just for the sake of it, these things become *your* personal experience. I might never trek the Kokoda trail or scale Mount Everest, but I can talk to people who have, read their stories, watch their documentaries and then, like taking a magic potion, their real, lived experiences, become my knowledge at some level. Being humble and just playing, being curious and just wanting to know things, all work together to make you a person with more personal experiences. This makes you more creative.

Albert Einstein, upheld as a creative scientific genius, is renowned for his playfulness and his relentless curiosity. He went so far as to say, 'I have no special talents. I am only passionately curious.' (in Irvine, 10)

Curiosity allows us to have a mind open to new things. Or, put it another way, a mind that loves to play with knowing new things. In fact, it is possibly the definition of a mind open to new things. And a mind open to new things is a powerful creative mind. It is also very important to note that being humble, as we looked at earlier, fits perfectly with your curiosity. Curiosity is about knowing that you don't know, but wanting to know. And that is a powerful thing. In his piece investigating intellectual humility, Stan Grierson makes the simple point that; 'Curious people tend to be intellectually humble.' (41)

Here's the real kicker for your creative life.

Curiosity is where all your ideas are going to come from. It's what Ernest Hemingway pointed to:

> A writer can be compared to a well. There are as many kinds of wells as there are writers. The important thing is to have good water in the well, and it is better to take a regular amount out than to pump the well dry and wait for it to refill. (13)

This is the very foundation of creativity, the beginning of everything. American poet Jack Gilbert notes that, 'You can't make a poem out of something that's not there. And it won't be there unless you want it to be there. And if you don't want it to be there, you're in trouble.' (455) The simple math is that you can't make something from nothing. So many highly successful creative minds have come to this same thought. Aussie rock legend Brian Cadd, who wrote *A little ray of sunshine* and founded Bootleg records, said that for him, creativity;

> comes from within you. And it's to do with the fact that our minds, our memories, are basically hard drives. They've got millions of things on them, things of the way you look, the way people's voices sound, things that they say and the colours of things. But it's fairly random access. A trigger mechanism will start the subconscious throwing stuff out. The trick of the songwriter is to be able to consciously assemble them into a song. As you write over the years you become able to do it. (114)

He calls it a hard drive, Hemingway and others call it the well, the muse, the inspiration. It's the same thing. Nick Cave is aware that,

> I'm taking everything in and my inspirations come from everywhere. They come from the good and the bad and the beautiful and the ugly and deeply flawed things and extraordinary things. They come from watching really bad movies, from watching really great movies [etc] So you absorb stuff without really realising it. (431)

The thread is common and powerful. To have creative output you must fill yourself with input. Truman Capote was asked if, as a novelist and journalist, he actually reads much.

> Too much. And anything, including labels and recipes and advertisements. I have a passion for newspapers – read all the New York dailies every day, and the Sunday edition, and several foreign magazines too... I average about five books a week. (26)

And on and on it goes. Because this is a truly important thing for all highly creative people. They fill their well. They absorb. They are relentlessly curious. We can only make from what we know. We imagine with images and ideas that already exist in our heads. This is the well. *You* are the well. You are a well-head.

The vital thing to note here is that curiosity, filling the well, is not just something you do. Just like play, curiosity is something you *are*. You are curious and that fills your well. Often untethered and uncontrolled. It's a lifestyle. You can't easily say 'I'm going to do some creating in an hour, so for the next hour I'll be curious.' The problem with that is that it pushes everything into the hands of executive control and away from the joy filled, playful, unrestrained passion of just being relentlessly curious. The metaphor might be that the technically curious, the executively curious, will pick up a textbook to deliberately learn of a topic. The childlike, playful curiosity chaser will just pick up the blob of playdough and feel it, see how it moves, marvel at the way it sticks to your fingerprints, the way it tastes... okay, that may be TOO curious, but you see the difference. Beautiful and powerful well-filling curiosity is vital for the creative mind. And it is done for its own sake. Hollywood film producer Brian Grazer says that 'Curiosity is itself a form of power, and also a form of courage.' (15) He goes on to note that,

> Good storytelling requires creativity and originality; it requires a real spark of inspiration. Where does the spark come from? I think curiosity is the flint from [which] flies the spark of inspiration. (35)

A word about...
The danger inside the Box

'Thinking outside the box' has become so much a part of modern culture that it is hard to see it as a myth. It's become the common short hand for 'Be Creative'. By doing so 'The Box' has become normalised, a standard thing that the world has to break out of.

But how did that happen? And why? Here's a fun game to play next time you're in a meeting where that phrase is bandied about. One of those 'Blue Sky', 'Brainstorming sessions' that companies use to try and reinvigorate their stale thinking.

The management man or woman stands before you in a cloud of parfum and fashionable shoes and says, 'I want you all to think outside the box.'

Stop them there. 'Excuse me, sorry to interrupt, but before we move on can you please explain what the box is that we are seeking to escape?'

Now, after some initial sighing, deep breaths etc., they will likely settle on a couple of things that will boil down to various versions of 'How we always do it,' 'Rusted on thinking,' 'Predictable responses' and 'Playing it safe.'

Thinking they are now over your impertinent speed bump, they will begin to launch into how they think you should think to 'think outside this box' they have so neatly delineated. But no, perfumed one, you don't get out of it that easily.

'Sorry, sorry again, but… this box. Can you please tell us; who created this box?'

You see, for management, this is the one question they rarely look at. WHY is this group of individuals thinking the same way, doing the same things, operating with rust and playing it safe? The reason, as everyone in the room should be able to see, is because that is how the company/group/team has always done it. It is the way things are managed. It is the culture. They may even call it their 'DNA', 'the way we are.' So, if your aftershave-soaked executive hasn't melted down but has been able to point out this situation, you can be a right proper smartass and ask them;

'So, in order to think outside the box, you are willing for us to unravel everything that the management of this company/group/team has relied on all these years, and define better ways of doing what we do?'

Which leaves everyone in the room with one last question. How often is the demand to 'Think outside the Box' shouted at us by the very instruments that built and maintain the box? And therefore, are we *really* safe to think outside of their box?

Getting comfortable with being curious is difficult in a world where we are expected to be constantly at work, always creating. But here's where it ties in with everything else we're looking at. Being the child, being the curious questioner of everything, is the basis of your creative power and it can be carried out as part of your 'down' time. I mentioned earlier how I will, after periods of intense creativity, expect to be 'down'. Physically and mentally exhausted from operating at a high level. So rather than grinding on, rather than sinking deeper into the mire of being down, I deliberately frame this time as well-filling. I call it absorbing. I will tell my wife, 'I didn't get much done today, I had a day of absorbing.' It is just as vital to my process as doing the actual thinking and writing work. If the well runs dry, I have nothing to give. So it's my job to ensure I wisely manage my well and its levels. Like a gardener of exquisite plants. The right mix of water, sun, rest, shade. And a bit of fertiliser.

Helen Garner speaks of how this well filling actually drives her inspirations.

> I read the paper and doors open in my head like those in a cuckoo clock. I had forgotten why people read papers. You learn things. Ideas come to you. Connections strike off each other with ringing blows or slot together like carpenters' joints. (7)

It's all coming together now.

We create and imagine freely and powerfully from a place of childlikeness. Why? Because it is unrestrained, fearless, humble and relentlessly curious. Nothing is bad, everything is possible, there is no judgement. Because you live a curious life, you have a well full of everything, so everything is there to play with. Children create from curiosity, to find out what the heck is going on, or just to see what happens. In his satirical novel *Still life with woodpecker*, Tom Robbins writes;

> Humans are the most advanced of Mammals – though a case could be made for the dolphins – because they seldom grow up... Humanity has advanced, when it has advanced, not because it has been sober, responsible,

> and cautious, but because it has been playful, rebellious and immature. (28-29)

But for this rebellious immaturity to become a useful product, for your curious imaginings to move into the world of reality, of day to day living, it requires executive control.

> Although creativity did lead to innovative performance, it also was associated with poor attention to detail and lower performance quality (e.g., being thorough and conscientious). Conformity, in contrast, was linked with higher performance Quality. (Kaufman, 158)

So if you're a pastor, or a teacher or a radio announcer, you can be as outrageously creative, rebellious, and immature as you want, so you can make amazing stuff. But you can also get sacked for not taking your audience with you, or not connecting, or just being too weird. As you develop your skills and excellence, in balance with this child like rebellious, immatureness, make sure you consider the other side of the see saw. The child on one side, the manager on the other. Remember when we were landing the plane, earlier? You want your pilot to have complete attentional control. But if you are creating the in-flight menu, maybe you could let go a bit and come up with something amazing and unique? Maybe something you saw in a documentary about play dough. Let the child play but also make sure the adult steps in and analyses, questions, probes and shapes the idea to make it valuable.

In the world of creative writing, we call that editing. Editing happens once a work has been created.

Finally, never forget this:

Play can be the heart of you just being. Unleashing. Getting out from under the restriction of adult executive control. Curiosity is the same. Finding interesting things just because they exist. You don't need to play or explore with a specific aim. But you *do* need to do it.

My wife has a cushion that has shaped my life. It says:

> Sometimes I just ride my bike to nowhere to see nothing
>
> just so I can ride my bike.

That is the essence of play. To just *be* the child with no specific aim. I ride my bike, not to get somewhere, not to train or develop. Just to ride my bike. We'll look a little more at why this is such a valuable creative superpower in the next chapter.

For now, know that when you want to create, you will thrive if you have previously set aside time to play. Then you can trust your knowledge and experience to just flow out of you.

In 1982, the zoologist George Bartholomew wrote:

> Creativity often appears to be some complex function of play ... related to the exuberant behavior of young animals. The most profoundly creative humans of course never lose this exuberant creativity. (In Bateson, 71)

You don't need to play or be curious to be creative; you need to play and be curious to be fully human. And you need to be fully human to be truly creative.

It All Boils Down to This:

Be the curious child.

- Play for its own sake is a wonderful thing.
- Curiosity for its own sake is a wonderful thing.
- Play is core to creativity. Sometimes it also helps when creating.
- The measurable is what gets managed. That does *not* make it more valuable, simply more visible.
- Being grownup can instil fear. Fear kills creativity.
- Being an adult is, however, vital to turning play into product.
- Curiosity is where your creative material comes from and will fill your well.
- The real power is knowing when to be the executive in control and when to be the child just squeezing the playdough.

Barnett, Lynn A. Playfulness: Definition design and measurement. *Play and Culture. 3*. Pp 319-336. 1990

Bateson, Patrick and Martin, Paul. *Play, Playfulness, Creativity and Innovation.* Cambridge. 2013

Capote, Truman. *The Paris review interviews Vol 1*. Picador. 2006

Case, Antonia. The Meaning of Intelligence. *New Philosopher.* No 40. Pp21-22. June 2023

Cave, Nick. *Songwriters speak. Conversations about creating music.* Krueger, Debbie. (ed) Limelight Press. Pp 415-427. 2005

Crabtree, Jeff and Julia. *Living with a creative Mind*. Zebra Collective. 2011.

Dahl, Roald. With Winkle, Justin. *The Pied Pipers.* Pp 101-112. Paddington press. 1973

Garner, Helen. *Yellow Notebook: Diaries volume one 1978-1987.* Text publishing. 2019

Gilbert, Jack. *The Paris review interviews Vol 1*. Picador. 2006

Grazer, Brian and Fishman, Charles. *A curious Mind: The Secret to a Bigger Life.* Simon and Schuster. 2015

Guralnick, Peter. *Looking to get Lost.* Little Brown. 2020

Hemingway, Ernest. *Ernest Hemingway: The last interview and other conversations.* Melville house. 2015

Irvine, Ben. *Einstein and the Art of Mindful Cycling.* Leaping Hare Press. London. 2018

Kaufman, James C. and Beghetto, Ronald A. Praise of Clark Kent: Creative Metacognition and the Importance of Teaching Kids When (Not) to Be Creative. *Roeper Review.* Vol 35. Pp 155–165. 2013

Kelley, Tom and Kelley, David. *Creative Confidence.* William Collins. 2013.

L'Engle, Madeleine. With Winkle, Justin in *The Pied Pipers.* Pp249-262. Paddington press. 1973

Levitt, S.D and Dubner, S.J. *Think like a freak. How to think smarter about just about everything.* Penguin. 2014.

Lubart, Todd I. and Georgsdottir, Asta. Creativity: Developmental and Cross-Cultural Issues in *Creativity: When East Meets West*. World Scientific, 2004.

Lumer, Ludovica and Oppenheim, Lois. A play of selves: Art as Play. In *For Want of Ambiguity: Order and Chaos in Art, Psychoanalysis, and Neuroscience.* Bloomsbury. 2019

Robbins, Tom. *Still life with woodpecker*. Corgi. 1980.

Robinson, Ted. *Do schools Kill Creativity.* https://youtu.be/iG9CE55wbtY 2007

Russ, S. W. Pretend play: Antecedent of adult creativity. In B. Barbot (Ed.), *Perspectives on creativity development. New Directions for Child and Adolescent Development.* Vol 151. Pp. 21–32. 2016

Santos, Sara, Sampaio, Jaime and Memmert, Daniel. Sports as a key route to ignite creativity. In *New Frontiers in Creativity*. Kreitler, Shulamith (ed) Nova science. 2020.

Sendak, Maurice. With Winkle, Justin in *The Pied Pipers.* Pp20-34. Paddington press. 1973.

Thorogood, George. And the destroyers. *Get a haircut*. Manning, Terry (prod). EMI America. 1993

Tyler, Jo A. What Really Happens When Adults Play? A Call for Examining the Intersection of Psychosocial Spaces, Group Energy, and Purposeful Play. *International Journal of Game-Based Learning*. Vol 7, No 3. July-September. 2017

Weisberg, R. The study of creativity: from genius to cognitive science. In *International Journal of Cultural Policy*. Vol 16, No 3. Pp 235-253. 2010

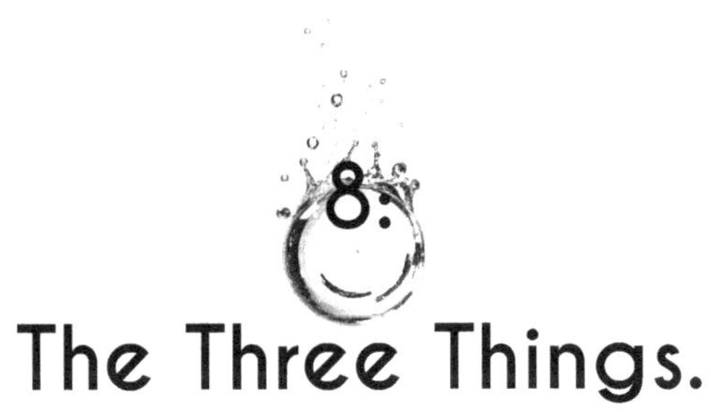

8: The Three Things.

Thing three:

The power of failure and being wrong.

> I've tried to keep my feet on the ground because otherwise someone is going to realise I'm a bit of a fraud. I've made no secret of the fact that I've been over-supported and given way too much respect. I've been given an easy life compared to others who deserved more and haven't had it. (in Kearns 8)

JONNY WILKINSON English rugby world cup winner.

When I came to write this chapter, I thought I knew why failure is such a good thing. I thought 'Yes, it knocks off the things that don't work, it helps us build resilience to be able to face all those issues that being creative incurs. And the secret is 'If at first you don't succeed, try and try again.'

But I was wrong. The more I looked back over this book and what I was learning from my students, from the research and from everything about creativity, it became clear to me that we misunderstand failure. It's not just the end point of a job. Failure is not only the fear that stops us. It is all of that, but also failure can be seen as the thing that ties all of our creativity together. Bear with me here. I need to put all the bits on the table, so you can see how they all fit together. So, quick review:

Wrong, ambiguous, and Imposter Syndrome

We know that being 'wrong' is a vital part of your creative life. We looked at it in terms of being humble. We looked at it in terms of being childlike. We looked at it as a basis of our curiosity. So rather than just thinking of 'wrong', which is often seen and felt as something negative, let me reframe 'wrong' as something powerful and useful.

'Wrong' is simple to understand. Wrong is easy to see. Before we finish the work it is always 'wrong'. Wrong is easy to measure. Wrong is what they don't like, what I don't like and what doesn't sell.

But what if wrong is simply:

Ambiguity.

Okay, oxymoron, 'simply Ambiguity,' because ambiguity is not so simple. It's a fairly complex concept. You could almost say that what ambiguity is, is ambiguous. But that is unhelpful. One dictionary definition is,

> (an example of) the fact of something having more than one possible meaning and therefore possibly causing confusion: (Dictionary.com)

Ambiguous is not the same as wrong. Wrong is when it's not right. Ambiguous is when it can be a whole lot of different things. The first band ever to play a punk song were wrong. But unambiguous. It was what it was, even if the world wasn't ready for it yet. Have you heard of the Pulitzer Prize winning novel *A Confederacy of Dunces*? In *The New Yorker,* in 2021, Tom Bissel wrote of '[author] John Kennedy Toole, one of the most famous "failures" in the history of American literature,' before explaining why and how his novel has become such a touchstone for much in American literature. He enumerates the flaws of both author and work, how it was 'wrong' but ends on the observation that;

> Early in the novel, [protagonist] Ignatius tells us, "I am an anachronism. People realize this and resent it." In 1968, Toole's hero mystified one of the country's finest editors of fiction. In 1980, he seemed harmless. Forty years later... Ignatius J. Reilly—the godfather of the Internet troll, the Abraham of neckbeards, the 4chan edgelord to

> rule them all—was no anachronism. He was a prediction. (Bissell)

All that wrong was now 'right'. What John Kennedy Toole wrote was wrong in many eyes but has now become a much loved... and much hated... novel. It is possibly the literary definition of ambiguity. But before Toole's mother pushed the novel into the world, it was ambiguous in a different way. Before a book is published it is ambiguous. It can be rewritten, edited, made 'right'. Or even more wrong, but it is in a state of ambiguity because it is unfinished. Even finished it can still be ambiguous, confusing and confused. And that's the takeaway for the creative individual. Being 'wrong' is *not* the same as the work being ambiguous. Wrong is things like bad spelling, clumsy and confusing grammar, mistakes and misattributions. Call them skill errors. But when finished it should not be 'wrong'. As a novelist, my novel will be ambiguous, having more than one possible story and meaning, until I have decided it is finished and my message is ready to go out. Of course, the beauty of art is that, even when it is completed and out there, it is *still* ambiguous. In some cases, ambiguous and wrong can be the same thing. For example, writing a murder mystery without clues or a resolution, is wrong. It won't fit the genre and readers won't 'get it'. My murder mystery with all this wrongness may not be wrong, it's just in the wrong genre. So it may just be ambiguous. But wrong for that specific genre. Same with romance. Or any literary genre. If it doesn't fit the genre rules it can be so ambiguous, so devoid of identifiable meaning, that it is 'wrong.' The way Nigel Kennedy plays the violin and the image he presents is very un-classical. So he is referred to as a punk violinist. Some would no doubt say that he is, therefore, wrong. Others will enjoy the ambiguity, the confusion, and just rock out.

Ambiguity and being wrong are vital to understand, because they are probably the reason most, I'll go so far as to say ALL highly creative people, in fact, all human people at some stage, to some degree, will get a dose of;

Imposter Syndrome.

When the work is in progress, therefore 'wrong', and you are faced with all the possibilities that this ambiguous state allows you, it can be very easy to believe that the way it is now is the way it will always be. This work, this task, my job, my dream, whatever, will never be what it could be because up 'til now I have been lucky, ridden the coat tails of others, or people are just blind to the fact that I can't do this. Why do I think that about myself? Well, look at this half-finished pile of steaming guano! It's wrong! Clearly, I am an imposter. Yes. And no. Let's unpack this a bit.

In 1978, When Pauline Clance and Suzanne Imes came up with the concept of Imposter Phenomenon, before it became a syndrome, they were examining a very new concept to science. Women get treated different to men. Their not unsurprising finding was that, after centuries of patriarchy, women didn't deal with being brilliant and successful the way men did. Okay, that's not how Clance and Imes put it, but you get the point. They spoke of;

> an internal experience of intellectual phoniness which appears to be particularly prevalent and intense among a select sample of high achieving women. (241)

The constant suppression of female excellence led to this thing within women that meant they felt that their success was not because of their own skill, talent, or excellence, but was caused by a mistake, a fluke, an anomaly. And the research has a very valuable point to make. Women suffer greatly as a result of their success being seen as questionable. Men less so. Clance and Imes do, however, make the point that 'we have found that the phenomenon occurs with much less frequency in men and that when it does occur, it is with much less intensity.' (241)

If this strikes a chord with you, go look at the original paper, it's a great piece of work. But we're not here to wrestle with gender issues or even with Imposter Syndrome itself. What I want us to do is see what lies under the construction we know as Imposter Syndrome and look at the pesky goblin there that is at the core of a lot of our creative failings. Susanne Fiegofsky points to the causes of Imposter Syndrome. From her list of five, I want to highlight these two because they seem to slap straight in the face of the creative thinker. Two mistakes we make that allow the imposter goblin within to scream at us that we are frauds and phonies:

> **(2) Natural genius:** They measure their competence by how easily any achievement/success comes to him/her. Hard work/perseverance are viewed negatively, as success should have come more easily.
>
> **(5) Soloist:** They measure competence by being successful on their own. Having to ask for help is considered a failure. (Fiegofsky, 861)

Does that sound like you? As mentioned earlier, writers and painters are particularly framed as 'soloists', working alone at their art and craft. Can you see that one working in your life? As a writer, if you need help, you are a failure. A phony. And to her other point, that you should find brilliance easy or you're a fake. If you have to work at creating genius, sweat at the canvas, grind out the work, you are an imposter. For all of us, the natural genius concept can be a real killer. You're not a natural genius like that guy on stage, effortlessly playing. So you're not good enough. Look at all the brilliant books in this bookshop, yours is a pile of disconnected notes, clearly you're not good like them. Your partially completed PhD thesis is nowhere near as concise and startling as the work you read in journals, so clearly, you're not good enough. You run this company do you?

Not as well as that company over there. Clearly, you're not good enough. You are, therefore, an imposter.

The obvious thing here, and I'm sure you've already seen it, is that these judgments are made of a completed work, an examination of a work or task that has undergone a lot of work and 'editing'. Unlike the work still clattering about, ambiguous and unfinished in your own head. And it is really important to get this sorted because, as Suzanne Fiegofsky goes on to say:

> Imposter Syndrome can have a negative impact on performance. Overpreparing, procrastinating, and working longer hours to avoid errors (or to prove competence) can increase rates of anxiety, depression, and burnout. (861)

Won't it be great to get to that point where you are so experienced and so successful that imposter syndrome just dissolves in a puff of logic?

Well, that's not going to happen.

At least, not without a lot of push from you. The really powerful observation in this research is that proof doesn't defuse Imposter Syndrome. As a new artist, as a young executive, as a beginner in your field there's probably a good argument that you feel 'not good enough' because, as yet, you're possibly not good enough. But Imposter Syndrome is the belief that you are not good enough, even though it is abundantly clear to everyone else that you *are* good enough. Writing in the *Evening Chronicle*, Imity Brighty-Potts points out that, 'Even the most talented, accomplished, experienced, educated, successful people have this experience.' And that seems to be borne out in the lives of highly effective people. Michelle Obama famously claimed that,

> I still have a little Imposter Syndrome, it never goes away, that you're actually listening to me. It doesn't go away, that feeling that you shouldn't take me that seriously. (in White, 31)

Hugely successful and adaptable writer Neil Gaiman has said that,

> The first problem of any kind of even limited success is the unshakeable conviction that you are getting away with something, and that any moment now they will discover you. It's Imposter Syndrome, something my wife Amanda [Palmer, the musician] christened the fraud police. (In white, 30)

Iconic Australian painter Gary Shead, winner of the 1992 Archibald prize, says,

> There have been times in my life when I've wondered whether I was in the wrong trade. But then my wife,

> Judith, says: "what else could you do? Be a plumber or a builder?" So I guess I can't do anything else. (In McDonald, 190)

Brilliant Australian author Helen Garner told her personal diary of various iterations of Imposter Syndrome. Such as,

> My intellectual equipment has gone rusty. And has never developed to its full strength in the first place. I get frightened when I think it might be too late. (21)

Or John Steinbeck who gave the world *The Grapes of Wrath* and so much more. He says of himself, 'I'm not a writer. I've been fooling myself and other people. I wish I were... no one else knows my lack of ability the way I do.' (in Holman, 19)

Obviously, I'm focusing on the artists here, but it's in every field, in every land, in every person at some stage. Even Margaret Chan, the 7th Director General of the World Health Organization from 2006-2017. She has said:

> There are an awful lot of people out there who think I'm an expert. How do these people believe all this about me? I'm so much more aware of all the things I don't know. (in Kearns, 5)

And the list of examples goes on. Ask any successful creator and, if they are honest, they will be able to point to at least a fringe of Imposter Syndrome. We all know that sneaky internal goblin.

So why is failing, why is imposter syndrome not a bad thing?

> It's also a safeguard against becoming arrogant, conceited, boastful or underprepared. (Brighty-Potts)

Imagine you are one of these creative stars and you carry on like you are as good as others think you are, swanning about like you are the be all and end all. Yes, there are some who do that, but they don't last long. Can you be a highly creative person for any period of time and be arrogant, conceited, boastful? I don't think so. We mentioned earlier how humility is vital to the creative process because it means you can develop and grow the work whilst still being supported, stable and reliant upon your own gifts, skills and domain excellence. The arrogant, boastful conceited ones will, however, never cope with being 'wrong'. They will never allow for another's brilliance to shine with them and lift them up.

A word about...
Functional Ambiguity.

This is a very helpful little phrase that has kept emerging when I have talked about the powerful creative life. It has also been central to how I am coming to know more about the God of creation. You see, like creating a work of art, our whole understanding of God, the universe, ourselves, everything, is growing out of a swirling pool of ambiguity. Of unknowingness. Anne Foerst notes that,

> 'ambiguity is imbedded in the texture of our life. Most complex phenomena, most of our urgent questions and ultimate concerns, and most of our sensory perceptions are inherently ambiguous.' (Foerst, 653)

So how do we get used to a life of ambiguity and why is it so hard? It's hard because ambiguity, like failure, is seen as being wrong. Peter McMahan wrote about just this problem. He stated that,

> 'Despite modernity's love affair with rationality and the precision that supports it, ambiguity persists not only in humour and politics but in all areas of contemporary life including scholarship and science.' (860)

So our modern world is increasingly looking for certainty, scientific fact and those measurables that make boardrooms and accountants squeal with glee. But even as rationality increases, the article points out that it is ambiguity, the unknowingness, that drives us forward. It is not certainty that makes humanity grow, but uncertainty. Comfort will not lead to great things, even worthwhile things. Only discomfort and ambiguity can do that. The concept of Functional Ambiguity is the idea in my creative head that what I'm doing is not yet done, not good enough, not finished, maybe never will be, but I know that if I stop, if my functioning in the creativity ends, then the ambiguity wins, and nothing grows from it. It is extremely valuable to recognise the ambiguity, name it. And claim it. Make the unknowingness of your creative work drive the process forward.

This concept of Functional Ambiguity has most powerfully driven my relationship with the word of God. Because I have no idea what it really means. Well, a little bit, but I'm learning every day, because I want to know more. Therefore, I have two choices. Know a little and be stuck there. Or know I don't know much and let the new discoveries inform what I think I believe. Bear with me here, because the bible is a beautiful portrait of Functional Ambiguity. It is a collection of different types of writing, made thousands of years ago for an oppressed people in a far-off land with a vastly different culture. As a white, 21st century Australian, I read of them being oppressed. Now, I am an oppressor. In the bible 'You' is collective, in my land, 'You' is self-referent and individual. For them sacrifice was central, for me it's a method of extending my salary. Anne Foerst added that,

> The understanding of the Bible as God's word and, yet, a collection of historical documents is ambiguous. And Christianity embraces as the founder of their religion a man, Jesus of Nazareth, who was never part of their religion but, rather, lived and died a Jew. (662)

And it goes on. This bible matters to me, but I just don't know it well. Much of it is totally ambiguous. But I explore it as a functional collection that teaches me. If I'm willing to let it be ambiguous. In my creativity, in my faith, in my relationships, in every aspect of my life, I find that now when I am lost, confused, or just haven't seen a way clear yet, I need to remind myself that this is not ignorance or failing, it is Ambiguity. More than that, it is Functional Ambiguity, so it's going somewhere. Probably somewhere new and totally unexpected.

Foerst, Anne. Ambiguity. *Crosscurrents.* Pp 653-665. December 2019

McMahan, Peter and Evans, James. Ambiguity and engagement. In *American Journal of Sociology.* Volume 124 number 3, pp 860-912. Nov 2018.

It comes to this.

You need to know you are not as good as you want to be.

You need to know you are not as bad as you think you may be.

Can there be an easy way to balance these two things?

Maybe. My favourite way of thinking of it is this:

The Ugly Baby Syndrome.

Newborn babies are ugly. A squished pickled walnut covered in blood and goo. No, don't get angry, I'm just being honest. At first they are just a mewling, squealing, demanding, poop machine, that looks like an extra in a movie about aliens. They are all work and not much else. Fortunately, newborn babies don't stay ugly for long, otherwise we might just leave them in the maternity ward and go home. But we don't. Why?

Well, hormones obviously help but, more importantly for this conversation, babies have enormous potential. They are the future. They can grow and become... anything. They are the ultimate ambiguity. If any human has a right to feel like they are an imposter, it's a baby. They are incapable, at this stage, of doing anything a successful human should be able to do, and yet we love them as little humans. More importantly, we commit to helping these little imposters grow, develop and 'become.' But we don't do it alone, hopefully. We have families, friends, schools, resources and research all aimed at helping our ugly baby become a fruitful, healthy, happy grown-up human being. But we all start as ugly babies.

So does every single piece of creativity. Every song, every novel, every building, every garden, every business, every... thing, began as a mess of stuff with potential. Until it was parented, guided and grown, usually by a whole lot of people, to become the thing we all admire.

Is that ugly newborn baby anything more than potential? Not really. Is it 'wrong'? Kind of. Is it ambiguous? Definitely. Is it an imposter? Not at all. It is a completely amazing human that is yet to realise it's phenomenal personal potential. Or work out how to use a toilet.

As a metaphor for the creative process, I have really come to enjoy the Ugly Baby. It is noisy, messy, unruly and inconvenient. Like my unedited writing. But it is a bundle of incredible potential. It can only reach that potential if I parent it well, guide it, shape and encourage it. I will also need a village to help me. I can create alone but I cannot, wisely or effectively, release my child into the world by myself. Also, I won't let my baby out into the world alone until it is grown enough. And finally, some children just don't reach the heights we parents had imagined for them. But we still love them and care about them. What does *that* look like for your creativity? How many songs have bands recorded and then left off the album because it was 'wrong'? How many works of art are left in the artist's workshop because they love them, but the gallery doesn't? I personally have a file of stories that I love, and loved writing, but no one will publish. They are no longer ugly babies, they are my beautiful children. Just because they haven't been 'successful' in the traditional sense doesn't make them 'wrong'. They just haven't left home yet.

In the interests of completeness, let me present another thought that explains this process, but without ugly babies. Richard Holman has written a book about metaphorically Slaying Creative Demons in which he notes the ugly baby syndrome as this:

> When a creative idea is just an idea, it's untainted by the prosaic demands of execution. It's soaring, beautiful, perfect. Naturally, you're afraid that if you try to bring that idea into being, you'll be faced with all kinds of practical challenges that must inevitably diminish it. (21)

Yep, I think we can all relate to that. It is the point at which we fear removing the ambiguity and replacing it with creative certainty. Creative certainty. Two words that should never be seen together. What it points to is this. A stage of 'wrong' and ambiguous are both things we deal with as creators, and you need to get comfortable with them. But what about failure? Can we be good with that?

Ambiguity and being 'wrong' are clearly different to failing. Failing is when it is so wrong and so ambiguous that no one wants a bar of it. Nigel Kennedy and John Kennedy Tool were both, eventually, successful. But many have been less appreciated. In fact, John Kennedy Toole took his own life before his book became a 'success'. In the process of creating anything you may feel like an imposter in that state of incompleteness, but at least you know why you feel like an imposter. What if the syndrome is right and you *are* an imposter? This is where the good of failure comes in. When you've done all you can, done your best, and it has failed.

There are multiple memes about cats hanging on, and you have to get up one more time than you fall down, and blah blah blah.

All that is true. But it also fails to capture the sheer value and brilliant quality of failure as a creative tool.

Charles Camarda was a NASA astronaut and is a senior advisor at the Johnson Space Centre. He flew in the shuttle mission straight AFTER the disaster in 2003, which destroyed the shuttle Columbia and the lives of all aboard during re-entry. If you want to make sure lessons have been learned from failure, that's an object lesson right there. He lived. He said:

> Failure is so important to what we do, yet we beat it out of the children at school; they have to get only one answer and it's this answer, that's the correct answer... life isn't like that. Most problems that we solve have many solutions, and there are ways to fail. (In Lewis, 114)

Straight away I know most of us have flicked back a few pages to the idea that childlikeness and creativity is also beaten out of school kids. And now failure is being rejected too! Honestly, what are we doing to school kids?

Leave that thought there and let's see if there is some validity to what Charles Camarda says.

Is failure really that useful?

The possibility of failure can be the point at which you decide to fall for the fear and back out. Or take the fear on and, hopefully, create something stunning. Novelist Charlotte Wood suggests that;

> we fear and actively work to reject creativity when we see it. Even if we insist otherwise, what we actually want is replication of established, previously approved forms of 'originality'. We don't want truly creative stuff in our lives, our homes or our workplaces, because it is too risky, always on the knife-edge of failure. It's new by definition, and thus unknown. The unknown is always a threat. (Luminous 110-111)

Threat is a driver of fear. The fear of failing can be debilitating or, as many creatives find, it can become a driving force. Singer, musician and entrepreneur Chris Falson, says that, 'Without the possibility of failing, I think for me, the joy of doing a thing is gone.' (in Crabtree, 292)

Highly creative people will embrace that same tension. Failing is bad, but just creating the same old crap is even worse. To be highly creative is to push the bounds of failure, to carry wrong and ambiguity lightly, knowing that with them you can make something truly unique. When we were looking at play, and why that is so important to you and your creative life, we looked at some work from Patrick Bateson and his people. Well, here they are again, tying failure and play together:

> Immediate success or failure are irrelevant to the [play] activity, at least while it is in progress. The essence of play involves entering many blind alleys that often lead nowhere but occasionally lead somewhere really interesting. (99)

This is the vital point, I think. Play leads to interesting stuff. Failure is not even a consideration. Why should it be? We're just playing.

This works. I do this when I'm writing a novel, or even this book. I'm not trying to write something successful. I'm not even writing to get it published, not yet. Right now, as I sit in a noisy café in the weeks before Christmas, I'm just playing. I'm shuffling ideas around, I'm slotting in thoughts, making connections to other things. Playing. Am I failing? Not yet. Will I fail? Maybe. But if I focus on *that* I'll never finish this, and you'll never read it, and this will all be irrelevant.

Ambiguity is having a wide range of possible options. A confusion of potential if you like. Ambiguity is not 'wrong', not yet. Nor is it right. Failure, however, is the end result of a process that hasn't worked. But is it bad?

Not as such. Beyond all the cat memes etc., It's time to point out;

Why failing is actually good.

Failure changes how you see yourself. Sometimes this can be debilitating and destructive. "I have failed; therefore, I am a failure." That's the bad way of carrying your failure. Internalising it and making it who you are. But what else can failure do? It can, and will, make you humble. I am not perfect. I am capable of failure. So what? So now, since you are humble, you can allow *more* creativity in. If you see yourself as a failure, you will contract and let in *less* creativity and freedom, because you blame that freedom, that ambiguity for your failure. You will fear it. But what if failing always allows you to see yourself as a humble creator in progress? What if failing *drives* you back to your childlike state of free, relentless creativity? What if failure is the speedbump that jolts you out of the rut and into the sky? What if failure is simply potty training your ugly baby? Fearlessly.

The general theory is that you only fail if you stop trying to succeed. But surely that is only half of the equation. You only fail if you stop trying to be better as you continue. Failure certainly forces you to grow if you allow it to drive you back to the heart of your creative joy. If the waves of the world dump you on the beach, make sandcastles. Play in the sand. Don't stop. 'Be Creative'. Fearlessly.

Failure will hurt and be uncomfortable. Yep. True. But the opposite is comfort. And comfort never created anything new. Failure hurts and brings all your beliefs about yourself and your creativity into question. But isn't that a good thing? We've explored how many of our beliefs about what we do and why, can be unhelpful. From cultural expectations to parental and societal rules, those hidden blocks and choke points. Maybe failure is the demand to drop all that crap and just be the creative child you are meant to be? Stop trying so hard to be something else and just be your free thinking, mind roaming, self.

Ah, self. Yes. Self. The one person who will always get in your way. The one who can't believe you no matter how good you are. Even when you don't fail, there is you, getting in your own way. The one that failure shines a light on. Your goblin of self.

Chris Hemsworth gets to be the god Thor on screen. That's got to be good for your ego right? But he notes that:

> The biggest lessons for me have always come from the hardest times… if you want to build a stronger character then you've got to confront your demons. You've got to confront those things that make you uncomfortable and learn to exist in that space. (71)

M.G. Vessanji, a Canadian novelist born in Kenya, puts it very succinctly, as you'd expect from a writer; 'If I can be rash for a moment, I think ambiguity is the driving force or the nuclear reaction behind my creativity.' (In Desai,190)

Wrongness, ambiguity, imposter syndrome, failure, are all very different, with a vast array of causes. But the response in our lives is pretty much universal.

Fear.

Our response to all of them needs to be variations on the same theme. Don't stop. Don't freeze, don't fear. Fly. Develop the habit of turning these things to your advantage. When the creative process makes you fear, when you fail by whatever measure you use, don't hide under the blankets. Make a cubby house and play there. Courage, it has been said, is not the absence of fear, it is the art of going on strong even in the face of fear. And yes, it's a habit. Developed by doing.

Remember earlier, Jerry Saltz told us how many artists;

> have tried every conceivable way to conquer work-block – that fear of working, which is a fear of failure. There's only one method that works: just work. And keep working… work is the only thing that banishes the curse of fear. (19)

The habit of working, of using your gifts to keep creating, that creates the habit of being creative. I love how this attitude to taking on fear head-on is not only extremely powerful but also continues across arts, across professions and ages and eras. You are not alone, you are not a freak, you are a highly powerful creative individual. Unless you choose not to be.

Unless you are fearful. And your creative excellence can be driven headlong by failure and by wrestling with your fear. No matter what. This is even applied to football players.

> "If you can take the time to understand fear, you can use it," says successful NFL player Lynn Swann. "I was always a little afraid in each game I played. Afraid of failure, of letting my teammates down, and of being hurt. I used that fear to make me a better player." (In Case)

After all of this, let me now prove I am NOT a visual artist, by trying to put together a representation of how creativity might work.

The Loopyness of Creativity

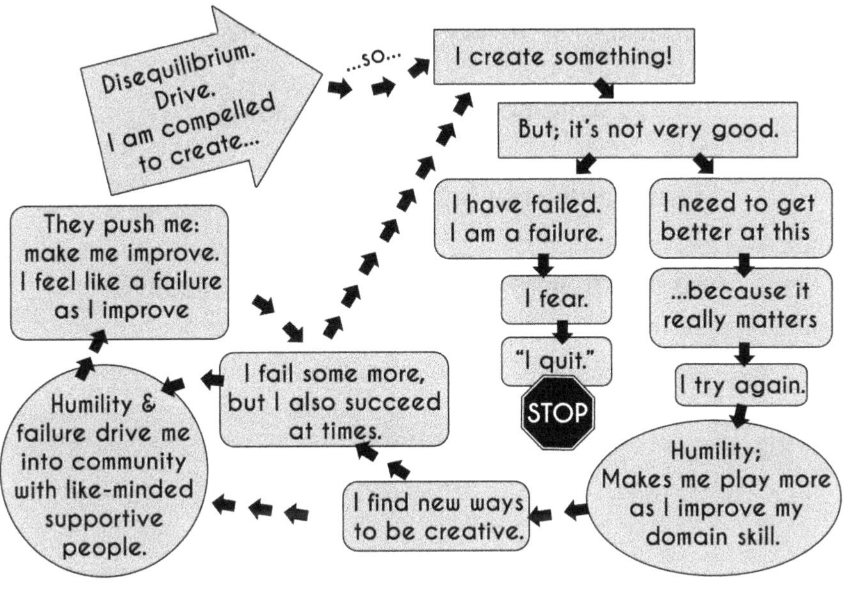

Creating is a job. Hard work. But also a joy, my reason for being.

A final word:

I love being creative.

I read because I love writing.

I write because I love reading.

I read and write because I love exploring.

And that makes me more and more creative.

References:

Ambiguity, definition. https://dictionary.cambridge.org/

Bateson, Patrick and Martin, Paul. *Play, Playfulness, Creativity and Innovation*. Cambridge. 2013

Brighty-Potts, Imity. How to recognise and tackle 'imposter syndrome.' *Evening Chronicle.* Newcastle, England. 11 July. 2023

Case, Antonia. Befriending fear. *New Philosopher.* p. 22. Nov. 2022,

Clance, Pauline Rose, and Imes, Suzanne Ament. The Imposter Phenomenon in High Achieving Women: Dynamics and Therapeutic intervention. *Psychotherapy Theory, Research and Practice.* Vol 15, No 3, Fall. 1978

Crabtree, Jeff and Julia. Living with a creative Mind. Zebra Collective. 2011

Desai, Gurav. Ambiguity is the driving force or nuclear reaction behind my creativity: An E-conversation with M.G. Vassanji. *Research in African Literatures.* Vol 42, No 3. 2011

Feigofsky, Suzanne. Imposter Syndrome. *Heart Rhythm Case Reports.* Vol 8, No 12. December. 2022

Garner, Helen. *Yellow Notebook: Diaries volume one 1978-1987.* Text publishing. 2019

Holman, Richard. *Creative Demons and how to slay them.* Thames and Hudson. 2022.

Hemsworth, Chris. Rolling Thunder, by Jhotty, Ben. *Australian Men's health.* Pp 64-71 March. 2021

Kearns, Hugh. *The Imposter syndrome.* Thinkwell. 2015

Lewis, Ben. Charles Camarda: why we need to fail to succeed. *Cosmos* No 84, p114. Sept. 2019

McDonald, John. *Studio: Australian painters on the nature of creativity.* R. Ian Lloyd Productions. Tower Books. 2007.

Saltz, Jerry. *How to be an artist.* Hachette. 2020

White, Cathy. The great pretender. *Writing Magazine*. Pp 30-31. June 2021

Woods, Charlotte. *The Luminous solution* Allen and Unwin. 2021

www.ingramcontent.com/pod-product-compliance
Ingram Content Group UK Ltd.
Pitfield, Milton Keynes, MK11 3LW, UK
UKHW020419250726
13967UKWH00007B/2715

9 780645 999174